'Do not ask WHAT MOVES ME SO PROFOUNDLY'

The ballad poetry of Annette von Droste-Hülshoff,
with translations into English and introductions

MARION TYMMS

'Do not ask WHAT MOVES ME SO PROFOUNDLY'

The ballad poetry of Annette von Droste-Hülshoff,
with translations into English and introductions

MEMOIRS
Cirencester

Published by Memoirs

MEMOIRS
PUBLISHING

1A The Wool Market Cirencester Gloucestershire, GL7 2PR
info@memoirsbooks.co.uk www.memoirspublishing.com

Printed in England

For Jo, as always!

ACKNOWLEDGEMENTS

I am most grateful to Tony Tingle and his colleagues at Memoirs for accepting my books on Annette von Droste-Hülshoff into their list and thus enabling me to fulfil a long-held ambition of making her work more widely known to readers of English.

In particular, I much appreciate all the work done by Chris Newton, Editor-in-Chief. Apart from his professional expertise, I have greatly valued his unfailing courtesy and good nature in handling some tricky textual issues, as well as a fairly opinionated client.

Ray Lipscombe has once again produced a striking and very appropriate cover, and he has ensured in his presentation of the text that these three books - despite their shortcomings, for which I alone am responsible - may encourage readers to explore the unique quality of Droste-Hülshoff's poetry.

Finally, my thanks go to my friend Robin Williams for allowing us to use his photograph, which expresses so exactly the bleakness and ambiguity of many of these ballads.

MET

CONTENTS

✤

CHAPTER I

※

INTRODUCTION TO ANNETTE VON DROSTE-HÜLSHOFF AND HER NARRATIVE POETRY

In 1993 Annette von Droste-Hülshoff was depicted on the 20DM banknote. In the same decade a similar honour was accorded to Bettina von Arnim (in 1991) and to Clara Schumann (in 1996). All three women had made significant contributions to the artistic life of Germany in the 19th Century, and it is possible that Droste-Hülshoff would have seen this as a sign that she had, after all, achieved her often-quoted ambition of being famous, not in her own lifetime, but through her writings a hundred years after her death. In this respect, as in so many others, she differs markedly from the other two women, whose names were fairly well known during their lifetimes, though their range and impact were ultimately more limited than hers. All three belong to an age of great creativity in Germany, but it is Annette von Droste-Hülshoff whose reputation has grown in the past one hundred and fifty years and allowed her to achieve a status commensurate with the range of her writings and, above all, with her extraordinary originality.

This is the third volume devoted to her poetic writings

1

published by Memoirs. As such, it adds another piece to the impressive jigsaw of her poetic achievement, and, as before, the intention is to make her work known to readers with little or no German. The translations attempt to resemble the pattern of the original on the page, but they are unashamedly in prose, with no attempt to copy the rhyme and metre of the German. This is, of course, a limitation of which the translator is fully aware, but it is hoped that the language is true to the original and that the qualities which characterize Droste-Hülshoff's writing - its sounds and cadences - are retained and do it justice, and give the reader a sense of its essence.

On the banknote already referred to, the picture of Annette von Droste-Hülshoff in early middle age is accompanied by a number of motifs which will have struck a chord with many of the population in the late 20th Century in Germany - an open book, a quill pen and, perhaps most tellingly, a tree. It is her *Novelle, Die Judenbuche,* ('The Jew's Beech') which is best known among her works, in Germany and beyond. This is the only work of prose fiction which she completed, and it occupied her for many years. It was published during her lifetime, to considerable acclaim, and it remains today the work of hers which can prompt a response in most Germans of average education and, more widely, through the many translations. It has been the object of much discussion and analysis, by schoolchildren and university students, and by literary critics who have occupied themselves with her and with her place in European literature. It may be the single work for which she is best known, but when it is considered in relation to her whole complex oeuvre, it also emerges as significant in a broader way, taking its place among the poetry for which she may be less well known but which also points the way to an understanding of her whole fascinating and diverse work.

While many highlight *Die Judenbuche* as her most important achievement, others see the religious poems contained in the cycle 'The Spiritual Year' (*Das geistliche Jahr*) as central to an understanding of her place in the literature not only of Germany but of Europe in the 19th Century, and a vital key to an insight into her thought. For others, her greatest achievement is in her lyric poems, some tentative and derivative in her early years, but coming to a remarkable peak in the many poems she wrote in the final decade of her short life. The truth is probably easier to identify, and it exists in the fact that her work is a remarkable whole in which the pieces come together and proclaim a very great talent.

Thus we come to the narrative poems to which this volume is devoted and realize that they, too, could claim to be a peak of her achievement but that, much more than that, they are an essential part of the whole. Indeed, to exclude this large corpus of poems would be to distort the picture of Droste-Hülshoff's achievement and ignore her originality over a variety of genres, and the scope of her genius.

A charming drawing by a close contemporary of hers, the artist Theodor von Oer (1807-1885), is reproduced in Peter Berglar's volume *Droste-Hülshoff*, (p. 78) and shows an animated young woman at a window entertaining a group of children with her story-telling. We know that, with her sister Jenny, she contributed to the famous collection of fairy-tales by the Brothers Grimm, who were regular visitors to the household as the girls were growing up. She was clearly fascinated by narrative, and, as with most of her enthusiasms, this one must have endured throughout her life, changing from the stories told in the Hülshoff household during the long winter evenings to entertain her family and friends, to the long ballad-like poems to which this volume is devoted, and of course, to the famed story of Friedrich Mergel and his terrible end in the beech-tree.

One sometimes finds oneself resorting to circumlocutions like 'balladesque' and 'ballad-like' because the poems considered here do not conform to the norms expected of a 'ballad' even though most scholars writing about them use the term, and she herself referred seemingly without question to her 'ballads' and her 'ballad-years'. The huge volume entitled *Deutsches Balladenbuch* contains not one example by her, but then when it appeared in 1852 she was still very little known. More relevantly, however, the poems by her traditionally grouped under this heading rarely contain, either in theme or manner, the components one might expect of a ballad. They lack for the most part the kind of almost facile, folk-song material, and the rhythmic, easy lilt, aided by refrains and repetitions. This is simply not her style, or her taste, although she was undoubtedly familiar with these ingredients and enjoyed them, and probably delivered them with some expertise and gusto. In such matters, as in all else, Annette von Droste-Hülshoff goes her own way, uninhibited by conventions or accepted designations. Just as one struggles to define *Die Judenbuche* as a *Novelle*, though it usually passes for one, it is hardly possible to find a narrative poem that resembles one's idea of a ballad. She defies categorization, and that is a major part of what fascinates in her.

In her generally well-informed and perceptive book on Annette von Droste-Hülshoff, which probably remains the most useful introduction for readers of English, Margaret Mare makes a series of statements which are daring and questionable and, in the context of Droste-Hülshoff, almost alarmingly provocative. 'Ballads are a type of literature accessible to those who do not care for poetry which makes too great demands on the imaginative and critical faculties' she writes (p.151) and goes on to ask: 'Why is it, then, that so few of Annette von Droste-Hülshoff's ballads are known to a wide public, even in Germany?' One could answer this question by saying that Annette von Droste-Hülshoff is not *widely* known at all, though this situation has changed and will doubtless continue to change. However, Margaret Mare adds to the contradictions when she asserts: 'As a writer of ballads Annette von Droste takes a high place in a literature rich in them' and in a sense she is right, but the problem arises when one seeks to compare her poems with the traditional examples of her Romantic predecessors - Uhland, Brentano, Eichendorff, for example - or of Goethe and Schiller, who, in the very year of her birth (1797), had designated a whole year their 'Ballad Year' and had produced a corpus of poems which tended to define the genre in German literature.

Droste-Hülshoff used the term 'ballad' to describe some of her poems and even spoke of her own 'ballad year' which spanned the beginning of 1840 to August 1841, and if, as is customary, critics adopt the term, it is in the knowledge that it is probably the simplest way to describe a kind of poetry at which she excelled, not conforming to any norms and rejecting accepted conventions. It serves in this volume for want of a better word, and always with the awareness that in this realm, as in so many others, she stands alone. Not included here, for obvious reasons of space but mostly because they belong under a quite different heading, are the three long epic poems based on historical sources that she had produced at a relatively early stage of her career and which appeared in her first published volume of 1838: 'The Hospice on the Great St Bernhard Pass', 'The Doctor's Legacy' and 'The Battle of Loener Bruch'. These are powerful narratives which warrant separate consideration, and translation by another hand, but they belong in a totally different category. Only one poem is included here which does not conform by any stretch of the use of the term 'ballad' and that is 'The City and the Cathedral', but, side by side with its counterpart 'Meister Gerhard of Cologne', it shows the extraordinary flexibility of her imagination and her writing and seems to justify a place here.

Before passing to what is the core of this book, the poems themselves, it is perhaps appropriate to refer to its title, the long and puzzling admonition which is actually the first line of one of her poems to her dear friend, her lover perhaps, the writer and critic Levin Schücking. She urges him not to ask what it is that moves her so profoundly when she gazes into his eyes, and it seems that a similar awareness of a barely identifiable emotion is often present in these poems. As one reads them, even with the limitations of a translation, one is aware of the depth of her involvement, the profound sadness very often, which seems to inform her choice of substance and her treatment of it. She understands grief in all its intensity, and she conveys it in a way which takes her reader along with her to a similar experience. The poems have at their core stories told with drama and passion, but, much more than that, they tell of the capacity of the human heart and mind to endure the sharpest pain and often, in the end, to accept it. These are elements of the poems which follow that may not emerge immediately, or in response to individual examples, but, taken together, they contribute to the impact of this aspect of her work. It is this feature that moves one so profoundly, as it surely must have moved Annette von Droste-Hülshoff herself, for the most part towards the end of her troubled and often anguished life.

CHAPTER II

❧

HER FIRST BALLAD: 'EMMA UND EDGAR'

As early as 1810, the thirteen-year-old Annette von Droste-Hülshoff composed a ballad, 'Emma und Edgar'. It is hardly surprising that, growing up in an aristocratic household, where reading was a part of everyday life, and she was already deep in the writings of Goethe and Schiller, she should have adopted the ballad mode. This youthful attempt, which shows all the signs of an acquaintance with the famous 'Lenore' by Gottfried August Bürger (1747-1794), is a respectable start. Highly derivative in theme and manner, it remained in manuscript form until it appeared in Wilhelm Kreiten's edition of her works (1884-87). It is not surprising that she did not seek to publish it during her lifetime, and it is omitted from the editions by Levin Schücking which followed her death. Subsequent editors have mostly also disregarded it.

Interestingly, it does make a brief appearance in her one attempt at 'comedy', the single-act *Perdu* of 1840. Here the final strophe of 'Emma und Edgar' is quoted in fragmented lines by the would-be poet Claudine Briesen, and in this context one may probably see it assigned by Droste-Hülshoff herself to where she felt it belonged, as a slightly pretentious youthful effort long superseded and better forgotten.

It is offered here because it is such a very early attempt by someone who was going to make the ballad type of poem very much her own in the years which followed, and because, derivative though it may be, it contains just the slightest hint of the direction she would take, and the originality that the years would bring. It deserves a place in the consideration of the development of a talent which, even at this early age, was feeling its way, and of a young woman who tried her hand at an extraordinary range of substance and manner as she moved towards the blossoming of her genius.

Emma and Edgar

The storm was raging though the forests
The rain was gushing down,
Soaking the waving fields
And hurtling down from the mountainside
The clouds were flying, the north wind blowing
Its way through the high vaulting of the castle
And Emma sat in her lonely room
And wrung her hands, weeping, in her grief.

The highest and the best
Her only possession and the greatest thing to her
Pure and tender heart
Had gone for ever
In the chaos of the blood and murder in the grass,
Where the raging battle had consumed him,

Edgar, to whom her heart had surrendered,
Her most precious jewel, her very life.

The bold warrior fell
In the savage tumult of the battle.
He fell a hero and a victor.
The night of death cast its shadow on him
And once more his gaze turned lovingly
Towards his homeland
And swiftly the deep breaths of life
Fled up into the air.

And his waiting bride
Was eagerly watching from the top of the high terrace
To see the beloved face
From her elevated seat,
And where normally the fleeting dance of the hours
Enveloped the lovely maiden in her bridal garland,
Now the minutes became hours
Dragging the weary seconds behind them.

The shadows stretched down
From the nearby ruins of the castle on the cliff-top.
The sun sank blood-red,
And the waves of the sea, its grave, turned crimson.
Gentle dusk spread over the meadow
And deathly silence reigned over the whole of nature.
Only the owl gave out his murmuring call
From the barren ruins of the castle on the cliff-top

And listen! It sounds like horses' hooves
Coming down from the mountain through the dark.
The earth is trembling, and the battlements are sending
The sound thundering back again.
Clouds of dust are rolling up.
The comrades are coming home laden with their prey
But ah! The biggest, boldest one is missing,
The bravest, best leader.

And she bows her head lovingly,
Down into the misty valley.
The heroes are coming thundering back,
And her heart is pounding joyfully at the sound.
But in the men's eyes is noble sadness,
And the warriors silently bring the corpse back
And hand him over to the faithful woman
To commend him to the bowels of the earth.

Emma hastens wildly
into the middle of the swarm of men.
And ah! Lying there in the midst of the warriors,
Pale and lifeless, is the precious face
And, horrified, endless pain takes hold of her
And in profound agony the loving heart lets out a sigh,
And wringing her lily-white hands aloft
She begs for her life to end.

Now after seven terrible days
The dark grave has concealed the beloved one.
The days have been filled with lamentation,

The nights with tears.
The clouds have flown, the north wind has blown
Through the high vaulting of the castle,
And Emma weeping in her lonely room
Has wrung her hands in grief.

And she hastens with faltering step
Down into the sepulchral vault.
Each muffled step echoes
down through the long halls
Cold midnight melts across the corridor
And all nature celebrates deep stillness
Solemnly the spirits climb from their chasms
out of the decaying tombs.

The trembling hand softly opens
The clinking bolts of the vaults
The door slowly creaks open
And her silken gown rustles as it flutters
And then the cold scent of the dead comes wafting to her
Through the wide open gateway.
But still she hastens with a bold step
Into the centre of the broad vault.

In wild anguish she sinks down
On the steps of the sarcophagus
To call forth the beloved life,
To warm the cold heart.
The wind whistles through the gap in the rocks.
The door creaks with the force of the storm

Softly the heavy bolt clinks,
Enveloped in waves of sea breezes

And behold, out of the chasms of the graves
Something rises up milky and white.
There's a swift buzzing in the dull air
And something hovers gently towards her
And it played about Emma's trembling hand
Which did not feel the airy kiss of the spirits.
She embraced the marble longingly
And covered Edgar's ashes with her tears.

At that the steps of the tomb quivered
And a long shadow rises up,
summoned by the tears of her devotion,
and approaches light and airy,
not surrounded as before in the radiance of his armour
Deathly pallor covered his handsome face
And beneath his heart
Yawned the gaping wound.

He pronounced these important words
"Emma, where the Judge resides
in the place of eternal recompense
faithful love is rewarded.
Therefore, be patient". He vanished as he spoke.
"Be patient" came after him a dull echo,
And the lid dropped down again
upon the marble of the tomb.

And now she sank down upon the grave
And embraced the cold stone,
Called back the shadow of her dear one,
begged for union with her beloved.
Fearfully the loving heart pounded within her bosom
And mortal anguish poured through her veins.
The loving, fleeing life barely
Hesitated with its fearful pounding.

The reddish glimmer of the morning
Was breaking through the awful darkness
And the gale still roared.
The rain was beating down
The clouds were fleeing and the north-wind still blew
Through the darkness of the sepulchral vault
And played gently round the pale,
Beloved, saintly corpse.

It is not enough to see this poem as a conventional ballad very much in the Romantic vein. The story of the mutual love of the young couple, Edgar's death in battle as a brave soldier and a leader of his men, and the grief of his waiting bride who succumbs when she cannot live without him, is told with considerable poignancy, but it avoids blatant sentimentality. What marks it out and anticipates some of the characteristic features of Droste-Hülshoff's mature narrative poems is the powerful evocation of the natural setting, the raging storm, the night with all its threat, the noises outside the castle where Emma waits and then grieves in desperate solitude. Above all, it is her brave venture to the vault where her dead lover has been buried which conveys the fear she experiences, yet her resolve. The description of the appearance of the ghost of Edgar is extraordinarily restrained and all the more powerful for that. He appears and disappears, leaving her with the reminder of the almighty Presence in the realm he now occupies, and the injunction to patience, which almost certainly echoes the similar phrase in Bürger's 'Lenore'. That she is dead when morning comes is shocking, but hardly a surprise. Had she not after all, 'begged for union with her beloved' the night before? Her urgent pleas had been coupled with the ceaseless pounding of her heart and the physical anguish coursing through her veins. When morning comes, the wind and the rain are unabated, but there is a dramatic change in the reddish glow in the sky, and the poem comes to its inevitable end with the concentration on the pale body of the young woman.

The young Droste-Hülshoff is already showing that she can achieve a powerful impact with the minimum of words carefully chosen, and with a subtle use of traditional ballad features, like the occasional repetitions of phrases and impressions. Even if it was more or less lost as other occupations took over, domestic duties and the enthusiasm she always seems to have felt to try her hand at a variety of genres, some unfinished, but always pressing their way towards a period of frenzied activity in her later years, this poem should not be dismissed but seen as a pointer towards what was to come, in her narrative prose, her attempts at drama, and above all in the magnificent lyric poems which mark the climax of her creative life.

As one comes to know and appreciate the remarkable ballads and other narrative poems she produced in the early 1840s, one should not forget this early effort, which displays so many of the hallmarks of her creative strength. Like them, it steers clear of the mawkishness which might have threatened it, and refrains from moralizing, and these are features which will become more and more evident as one proceeds to look at her later examples of this genre. It seems to have been a while before she produced anything comparable, occupied as she was by other ideas, and the four poems which follow here show the impact of new influences, and her extraordinary independence of the sources she selected.

CHAPTER III

✤

FOUR EARLY BALLADS: 'THE CHARIOT OF VENUS', 'THE COUNT OF THAL', 'THE FALL OF THE BARMECIDES', 'BAJAZET'

The years which followed this very early effort were undoubtedly full of new experiences for the young girl. Her family life in the Castle of Hülshoff was lively, with people coming and going, some of them distinguished socially and politically, and many of them influential in the cultural life of her time and her homeland, and she was already making acquaintances and friendships which were to influence her burgeoning literary talent. Although there is little to show now for what she produced during these years of her teens, one must assume that the family gatherings referred to in her own letters and the accounts of those who visited the family will often have been enhanced by her contributions as an accomplished pianist, an entertaining story-teller and a lively if sometimes rather gauche young member of a cultured family. During those years she read avidly and across a wide range and was well acquainted with the works of Goethe and Schiller, with the Romantic writers of

Germany and with classical literature and thought. From her father she developed a love of natural things, and her roots in the traditions and lore of her native Westphalia supplied a background which she used for much of her work. Throughout her life she felt herself firmly linked to the countryside and people around her, and by temperament she possessed the relationship with and understanding of the supernatural which characterised so many of her countrymen. This association was doubtless nurtured by her old nurse Maria Kathrin Plettendorf, who was her closest companion and dear friend for much of her life and who more than anyone furnished her with the superstitions and attitudes that found their way into so much of her writing.

During this second decade of her life she was always writing, demonstrating the disparate interests which remained with her until her death. She seems to have had the capacity to give herself with great enthusiasm to her ideas and to work with sometimes frenetic application. Thus these years saw a tragic drama, *Berta,* which remained uncompleted when she laid it aside in 1813, an epic in six cantos based on the exploits and soul-searching of a knight called Walter (1818), and *Ledwina,* her one and only attempt at a novel (1819) which did not progress beyond the draft stage but remains of interest, both as a further example of her interest in tackling a range of genres and for its manifestly autobiographical features. By the end of the decade she was deep in the spiritual poems which were to evolve into the cycle of poems *Das Geistliche Jahr* and eventually constitute one of her most significant achievements. By 1820 the first part of this cycle was complete.

At the same time as Droste-Hülshoff was demonstrating an

already remarkable scope in her choice of subject and mode, she was showing signs of the very poor health which would dog her footsteps throughout her life and must have impinged on her ability to achieve as much as she might have done. Her acute sensitivity was often accompanied by depression, but she was also suffering problems with her breathing and with her eyesight. Added to this was the event which in the opinion of some was to mark her emotional life for years to come, and perhaps for ever. Somewhat melodramatically referred to as 'the catastrophe of her youth', (her *Jugendkatastrophe*), this was the consequence of a youthful involvement with two young men simultaneously and might have been avoided by a woman of greater experience, or better judgement. For one who was clearly highly-strung and who lived on a high emotional plane, it proved very unfortunate to say the least, and meant that, after so much frenzied activity, she lapsed into what would doubtless now be described as a deep depression, full of self-reproach and unwilling to engage in much social interaction, or activity of any kind.

It may be that the poem which follows, a ballad which stands very much on its own, was the product of this time. Its dating is difficult, though it is sometimes placed as early as 1818, or as late as the beginning of the 1830s. We do know two things about it: that it was one of the poems which Droste-Hülshoff both wrote and herself set to music, and that she perhaps had some doubts about its quality. When she came to select poems for inclusion in her first published volume, in 1838, she offered it to the two friends who were responsible for the final selection (Christoph Bernhard Schlüter and Wilhelm Junkmann) and subsequently expressed her approval of their decision to reject it. The *Gräfin* ('Countess'), as she called it, did not fit in with the tone of the rest of the collection, which was 'consistently serious and simple'. Whether that was in fact the reason they omitted it is open to question, since they were altogether anxious to avoid anything that might be seen as 'strange or disturbing' (*fremdartig und störend*) in this first attempt by the aristocratic lady to present her work to the public. Its inclusion would almost certainly not have added to the success of a volume generally regarded as an unfortunate failure, the result of her own inexperience in presenting her work and the sometimes poor judgement of her friends, devoted advocates though they were. In the event, the one ballad included in that volume - 'The Count of Thal', which follows below - was received with considerable warmth.

That said, 'The Chariot of Venus' is important as an early attempt in a genre which was to become important to her and to her reputation. The setting of the court, the ambiguity of the love story it tells, the tragic ending which remains without comment and with no emphasis on the immorality involved, all these features suggest that she was again trying her hand at something new for her, though within an established tradition, while the knowledge that the piece doubtless entertained an audience at social gatherings in polite society with its pleasing piano accompaniment places it in a category of its own, though one that she would not pursue.

From the title on, there is an ambiguity and a certain flippancy about the poem. *Venuswagen* , 'Chariot of Venus', is a popular name given to a plant of the species of aconite, and it refers to the blossom which, with a certain amount of imagination, could be said to resemble the carriage of Venus, goddess of love, drawn by two doves, referred to in the fifth strophe. In English, popular nomenclature is darker: 'wolfsbane' and 'monkshood' reflect more sinister thinking, for many varieties of the plant are toxic. Droste-Hülshoff seems to have lighted on this plant, and given the poem its title, in order to express the duality of love, its beauty and its threat.

The insouciance of the noble lady sets the tone of the poem, for she is reckless, laughing scornfully as she bids farewell to the rose blossom as it drops in front of her. The situation is summed up in the briefest terms: it is night, her husband is fast asleep, and her lover has just left her. However, she knows the danger and can hardly comprehend her own behaviour. Nature seems to be passing comment, as the trees shake their heads, but then the other participant in this drama enters, the blossoming branch which mysteriously becomes entangled in her hair and brings its strange, ambiguous message. The threat is there, but almost immediately its retraction, and then the warning. Now there is no laughter, and the Countess displays all the signs of physical anguish, in fever and pallor.

The maid - surely not by chance called Lenore (see above p. 8) - arrives in a frenzy to deliver the summons from 'old Veit', and the description of his death throes supplies the link and the partial explanation of the branch with its telling flowers. How it came into his hand and on to his cheeks is irrelevant: what matters is that the old man has been the custodian of a secret which, if divulged, could have changed the course of events, but now it is too late. As the Countess removes the branch, she takes with her the knowledge that he shared her shameful secret but did not expose it. Her response is silence - no laughter now, no singing - and the poem ends in the only way possible, with her death, beautiful still, and clutching the branch with the now silent doves upon it, and the grief of her deceived husband. With the kind of sparse description which will become a hallmark of Droste-Hülshoff's work, not least her ballad poetry, the redness of dawn replaces the dark veil of the night. Questions remain, but it is not the business of the ballad to pose them, or to answer them, and the poet herself does not seek to point a moral.

The Chariot of Venus

A rose petal from the corsage of the noble lady
drops in front of her shoe, and she
laughs out into the night:
"God speed, my petal, God speed!" she says.
"Do not let that trouble you,
you flower of Love's desire:
you lie at my feet,
you lie upon my breast."

She speaks so wildly, laughs so scornfully,
and yet so softly and so gently.
(To be sure, her husband has long been sleeping.)
The castle stands pale and desolate.
Her lover has departed,
her cheek is burning.
What more does she desire?
Ah, that which she herself knows not!

"The cheerful little bird
has been imprisoned in a golden cage,
and now they are placing a net of roses round me

and I am boldly entering.
I must despise my husband
but, my sweetheart, do I love you?
I can never comprehend it,
so terrible it is."

The trees are shaking their heads silently,
the undergrowth is stirring,
and all at once a mass of blossoms,
stolen from the roots, is filling the air.
A Venus Carriage has become entangled
in her luxuriant curls:
"Ah, poor wretch, imprisoned!
Look how it hangs in chains!"

With her fingers ringed in gold
she releases the pair of doves,
and a buzzing like the singing of a gnat
can be heard through her hair:
"I could betray you" -
My God, who is that speaking? -
and then, as though through ears of corn,
comes the gentle sound: "But I shall not do it."

She shudders, and the flower falls,
"Step forward unpunished"
she boldly cries, her eyes blazing,
and the loud sound comes trembling up:
"Oh, my lady, turn, turn aside!"
The night of death burns,

the end is dark.
"My Jesus!" comes the groaning sound.

The countess moves her lovely lips,
and yet no laughter comes forth.
She wanders round the edge of the garden
and through the wooded parkland.
She tries to lift her head -
her brow is moist -
she stands and cannot tremble,
and yet she is so pale.

Then, like a flash of fire,
there echoes through those rooms:
"What is that light doing in my hall?"
The lady moves forward,
and then comes the sound of nervous footsteps
through the bank of flowers.
The lady knows the tread and calls:
"Lenore, I am here!"

"My God, how long you have been!"
she cries, still pale with fear.
"They are coming! Make haste, oh hurry!
They are looking for you at this very moment."
"What are they asking about?
What kind of emergency is there in the middle of the night?"
"Oh my lady, hear what there is to tell:
old Veit is dead!"

For a long time he lay in the throes of death,
sometimes he said not another word,
but then he cried out, as though in inner conflict,
so deep and hollow and loud:
"I must speak with the Countess:
oh, call her! wake her up!
My heart cannot break
until I do, my Jesus!" he groans out loud.

There was a dithering: they just stood there, stood there,
and then in a moment of madness
the withered, bony hand of the old man
grabbed at a branch of blossoms
which the storm had once broken,
and he spoke in a deranged whisper:
"You have never spoken,
yet you can understand me."

He looked at it with a profound gaze,
so long and so dreadfully,
and then softly spoke to himself,
and then lay still in deep thought.
And pressed it to his cheek:
"Maria! Queen of Heaven" he said.
"My God! how long, how long!"
His life was at an end.

What did the old man want?
"You never trusted him."
The Countess looks at her with icy gaze;

the maid is silent, full of fear.
"I wish to see the old man.
Lenore, follow me!"
And the two of them go through the darkness,
on and on.

Like a grey aloe,
broken by time,
his fixed stare directed upwards:
that was old Veit.
On his cheeks
the flowering doves flee away,
and little blue carriages
move past on the white background.

Who disturbed the procession of flowers?
Who led away a pair of doves?
There, where the blossom touches the dead mouth
as though in flight?
And if you had not been silent
seven moons ago, shyly, you
could have been victorious,
but now the time has passed.

The lady stares straight ahead,
to be sure, and yet she says not a word.
She takes the branch from his hand
and slowly walks away.
"You maids, loosen my veil!
My head is so heavy."

She plays with the lyre,
but she sings no more.

Do you wish to see the mistress?
Oh look! She lies there so lovely and so pale,
in her white hand
the mysterious blue branch.
The doves are silent.
The husband kneels and weeps,
and through the covering veil
the dawn appears.

If one places 'The Chariot of Venus', rejected for the first
publication of some of her early work, with the next ballad, 'The
Count of Thal' which did appear in 1838, one finds important
differences, yet some features which they have in common.
Moreover, from the beginning, it bears a likeness to the
traditional ballads with which Droste-Hülshoff would have been
familiar, with its four-lined strophe and rather simple rhythm.
What comes to mind readily is Goethe's 'Der König in Thule'
(1774) which opens:

Es war ein König in Thule,
Gar treu bis an das Grab,
Dem sterbend seine Buhle
Einen goldnen Becher gab.

(There was a king in Thule,
Totally devoted unto his death,
To whom his dying sweetheart
Gave a golden goblet.)

The opening strophes both introduce the two central characters, but there the likeness ends, even if the manner of the telling of the story is similar, and the traditional, archaic sound echoes in the later poem. Droste-Hülshoff's ballad tells a complex, tragic tale of marital love which presses the couple to the extreme, complicated as it is by issues of loyalty and honour, and by a hopeless dilemma whose only end can be death. It leaves the reader with many questions unanswered, and with issues of morality unresolved. It is, in fact, a far cry from Goethe's poem, which speaks of mutual love so deep that the golden goblet, the token of that love, must be hurled into the sea by the dying king who cannot bear to survive his beloved.

Droste-Hülshoff takes her material from an historical event with which her readers will have been familiar from Schiller's *Wilhelm Tell*. What she does with this material, however, is all her own, and her long ballad points the way to many other masterly examples of her skill in exploiting human situations and probing often dark dilemmas and complex motivation. The man at the heart of her story is Johann of Swabia, who makes a brief appearance in Schiller's drama of 1804, coming before Tell in the vain hope that he will find mercy and even forgiveness for his murder of his uncle, Emperor Albrecht I. The emphasis is different here, for she does not concern herself so much with the rights and wrongs of the act of a man who in 1308 had taken upon himself a dreadful deed which earned him the name of Parricida, as with the relationship between that man and his wife who overhears the plan for the assassination and from whom he extracts an oath of secrecy.

The last line sums up the tragic conflict of the woman: to prevent this terrible sin she must commit another, but in warning him, by carefully calculated and devious means, she demonstrates not the betrayal which angers him so much but her absolute love and devotion to him. Once more, the only end for her is death, and, as in 'The Chariot of Venus', Droste-Hülshoff does not seek to point a moral or to justify, still less to condemn.

The Count of Thal

It was the Count of Thal
who rode along the cliff-face.
It was his wedded wife
who stood behind the stone.

She gazed in the sunlight
down at the gentle slope.
"What has become of the Count of Thal?
Surely I can hear him riding along.

Is that the sound of horse's hooves?
Perhaps the distant sound of horse's hooves?
I know for sure without a doubt
That I have heard my lord approaching."

She bent the branch back and she said:
"Am I blind or deaf?"
She blinked into the bushes
and listened to the rustling of the leaves.

It was deserted in the cutting, empty,
lonely in the whispering forest,

and yet above the pond, on the embankment,
she soon came upon the Count.

She stepped into his shadow.
He and his companions
are whispering and conferring with one another,
and the waves are making a louder noise as they trickle down.

They stared across the land, peering
intently, peering,
and saw each little branch on the shore,
but not the lady on the embankment.

The Count glanced down and said,
the Count of Thal:
"For thirteen years shame unavenged
has robbed me of sleep.

Was that a soft sigh?
Comrades, who has heard it?"
Kurt spoke and said: "It is only the wind
blowing across the reeds."

"But I swear by the Almighty,
and if it were my wedded wife,
and if it were my brother's blood,
still less my own self:

nothing shall stop me taking revenge
on him - the bold man

shall be aware of this -
and with thirteen years' interest, too.

By God! What a groan that was!"
They exchanged swift glances,
and Kurt said:
"It is the Föhn making the branches of the pine-trees sigh."

"And even if his eyes are blind,
and even if his hair is grey,
and my wife the child of his sister!" -
At that the lady let out a cry.

The three men turned swiftly round
like weather-vanes.
"Stay back, stay back, my friend!
I am the judge of this woman.

Have you been listening, Allgund?
Do you say nothing, do you look down at the ground?
That will bring you a bitter hour!
Allgund: what did you hear? -

"I heard the sound of your horse,
I saw the light in your eyes,
as I came down the slope.
Now do what you have to do."

"Oh my lady," said Jacob Port.
"You are playing a dangerous game.

My lord has just said something
which presumed a lot."

Kurt said: "I'll tell you straight,
better the wolf in the stable
than the mouth of a woman
as a guard in such a case."

Then the Count looked at them,
at the one and at the two,
and the man said to the lady:
"I know for sure that you are mine.

When you lay around me in captivity
for a whole year
and spoke not a syllable,
I came to know your loyalty.

So swear to me here and now
that whatever you heard at the pond,
whether it was much or little,
is like mist and play to you,

as though nothing had happened,
I must believe that completely.
I must not see you weeping,
you must not come before me pale.

Think, think, Allgund,
what you must promise.

Your lips speak the truth,
I know that, and even if it meant death."

And if she could remember,
she had never promised it,
for she was only half- conscious:
she swore and knew not how.

II
And by the time the grey of morning
crept into her chamber,
the noble lady had already
sighed a few times,

wrung her hands many times over,
quite secretly, like a thief.
Her eyelids were red,
her sweet face deathly pale.

For three days she served the wine
and sat for three days at the table.
For three nights she lay in the forest chapel,
in unrelenting agony.

The gatekeeper sees her walking
when he is standing guard.
In the forest the poacher stands
and hears the groaning.

On the fourth evening
she was sitting at the side of her lord,
she turning her spinning-wheel, he reading,
when both of them looked up.

"Allgund, your lips are pale!"
"My lord, it is the lamplight doing that."
"Your eyes are red, Allgund!"
"Smoke from the fire has forced its way into them

and, also, it distresses me
that fifteen years ago today,
I saw my father's blood.
May God protect his soul!

My mother has long been lying in the Cathedral,
and I have few kinsmen left,
an aunt still, and an uncle,
otherwise I know no one."

The Count looked at her intently:
"A woman is steadfast
when she leaves her uncle and her father
for the sake of her wedded husband."

"Yes, my lord, it must be so.
For your sake I would give up both of them,
and myself too,
if it had to be, and without regret.

But, in order that this day
should not be the same as all the others,
may I ask you to read out
a short passage or two?"

And when thereupon
the lovely lady held out the Holy Book
to her husband,
it opened up of its own accord.

He cast a single glance over
one of the first passages and read:
"Revenge is mine".
That seemed strange to him.

Yet however intently the man
looked at his wife and at the Bible,
she sat there silently spinning,
and there was not a crease on the page.

Gravely he passed an arm,
around her lovely person:
"Now take up the lute, wife,
and sing me a cheerful song."

"Oh, my lord, if it pleases you,
I will sing a pious little song
that a minstrel taught me
only a few days ago."

He looked so tired and pale,
and only wished to rest a little,
and he said: "They say that in the upper kingdom[1]
they sing nothing else now."

Then, like a cry echoing out,
a sound goes through the chamber,
as her cold fingers
touch the strings.

"Johann, Johann,
what were you thinking
on that day when you slew your own peace of mind
with a single blow?
At the same time you brought grief upon
your three comrades.
Oh, look now at their pale limbs
swelling in the moonlight!

Woe to you, Johann!
Johann! what were you thinking about at that hour?
Now the news is travelling fast away from you,
you lost man, throughout the kingdom.
If the forest is to hide you,
you must make haste.
Just listen, the birds will soon be singing it,
the wolves howling it.

Oh woe! Johann, Johann,
you did not think of this

when you wrought
revenge upon the old man.
And woe! the curse
will never be buried with you,
you who murdered your uncle and your lord,
Johann of Swabia!"

The pale lady stood upright
before her husband,
who immediately seized the lute
and hurled it at the wall.

And when the sound was dying away,
his angry footsteps
could still be heard,
passing along the hallway.

III
Seven days from that day
it was a heavy hour
when Allgund lay on her knees
on the balcony.

Her heart was beating loudly:
"Oh, Lord, take pity on me,
and if I committed a wicked deed,
let the penance be mine alone!"

Then she bowed low,
listening, listening, listening.

A raging sound came down from the battlements.
It stormed down from the forest.

Was that a footstep? No!
A stag was crossing the ravine.
Was that a signal?
But no: it was the capercaillie calling.

"Oh my Saviour, my blessed one!
I am laden with sin.
Be merciful and take me,
before my husband returns home.

Alas, he whom the evil one seeks to beguile,
from him he takes all strength.
And yet I only warned him. I did not betray him,
Not betray him!

Alas: those are horse's hooves."
She saw them flying through the valley,
Riding wildly, grimly,
and she saw her husband, too.

She saw him threatening, distinctly
saw him clenching his fist,
and the lady's knees collapsed,
and she rolled over the edge.

And when, intent on a wicked deed,
the Count beat at the gate,

blood came towards him,
forcing its way out through the grille.

And when he saw his wife
clasping her hands in her last agony,
he could not hold back his fury,
and his flushed face turned ashen.

"Woman, who chose death for herself" -
"It was not my wish", she said,
hardly able to utter the words.
"Woman who broke her oath!"

Like the gentle breeze of eventide
she whispered again to him:
"A sin had to be committed,
and I committed it for you."

[1]'in the upper kingdom': ie in Austria

Although the slight volume published in 1838 did not receive much acclaim, this poem was singled out for warm comment, from her friends and the admittedly few critics who deigned to write about it. The reasons are not hard to find, and they point forward to the success she would gain as she developed within the genre. She takes a single historical event, and a known historical figure, and treats them with her characteristic understanding. The Parricida who, in Schiller's play, came to Wilhelm Tell aware of his guilt and seeking sanctuary, is different from the angry man who plots an act of revenge against the uncle who has deprived him of his birthright, but that difference is not her main concern. She shifts the emphasis to the relationship between the man and his wife, who has the misfortune to overhear his whispered conversation in the forest with his fellow conspirators. He knows from past experience that he can rely on her love and loyalty, but in this extreme circumstance he must be sure, or the whole plot will fail. Thus he demands that she swear an oath which, terrified and confused as she is, she barely registers.

Droste-Hülshoff conveys the transition from the dark night to the dawn which follows, bringing with it the woman's realization of what has happened, and the dilemma in which she is placed. Equally, she conveys the transition in terms of place, for the next conversation between the couple is in their home, where, away from the eyes and ears of his comrades, the woman decides to warn him in the most subtle, delicate way, utilising the normal accessories of everyday life, the bible and a little song she recalls hearing sung by a minstrel. He has, of course, his own terrible dilemma, and when he storms out, fully aware of what she has been telling him, the fate of them both is sealed. She dies, like the lady in 'The Chariot of Venus', but not out of shame or a broken-heart, but because the alternative will be to endure his anger. Again, Droste-Hülshoff does not engage in discussion of the rights and wrongs but leaves her poem on the poignant cry of the wife who states what we must know: that her motivation was her love for him and her loyalty towards him.

The details of this poem - the natural setting, the suspense, the small indications of time and place - are the kind of features at which Droste-Hülshoff will excel in her later ballads and in her lyrics, and, of course, in 'The Jew's Beech'. Beyond that, she shows herself adept at conveying human emotions and human dilemmas, as she will increasingly as her poetic strengths develop.

* * *

These two poems show already the way in which Annette von Droste-Hülshoff took her inspiration from diverse sources, in these cases a lovely plant with a known propensity to poison and a small scene in a great drama. It is on the basis of such relatively small hints that she builds a narrative all her own, and this we shall see her doing throughout the corpus of ballads and ballad-like poems which she was on the brink of producing with increasing skill. Sometimes she took up a small feature of the life she knew well, a superstition or a local anecdote, and sometimes her impetus came from a piece of writing she had chanced upon in her copious reading and listening in the libraries of her father and her uncles. One has the impression of a mind alert and receptive, and capable of adapting throughout her life. If one places these qualities beside the obvious sharpness of her intellect, one can see how, deeply immersed in the language and literature of her time, she was so very original, unbound by traditions and movements, however much she may have revered them.

A specific influence came into her life in the mid-1830s and led to the two poems which follow in this group, at the time when she was deciding which of her works she should put forward for inclusion in the volume being prepared for publication on her behalf by her friends Christoph Bernhard Schlüter and Wilhelm Junkmann. She had become keenly interested in Oriental literature through her reading of the work of Joseph Freiherr von Hammer-Purgstall (1774-1856). He had published prolifically in the literature and history of Persia and had, in fact, provided the material for Goethe's *Westöstlicher Divan* (1818) through his great translation of Hafez. Undoubtedly this will have had a place in the library at Hülshoff, but many years later, in a letter of February 1844, she wrote specifically to her friend Levin Schücking of her reading of Hammer-Purgstall's volume of translations of Persian literature with the extravagant title *Rosenöl* ('Attar of Roses'), telling him that her uncles had owned a copy. It was typical of the young Droste-Hülshoff that she should have read this exotic literature with some enthusiasm and found embedded in its stories germs of ideas which she could take up herself. The immediate result was the two poems included below - 'The Fall of the Barmecides' and 'Bajazet' - which added to the range of what may be described as her ballads, but much later these were to appear as the first poems in a group entitled 'Sounds from the Orient' (*Klänge aus dem Orient*), evidently following in the tradition of Goethe and his contemporaries. Although this group of poems was available for inclusion in the 1838 volume, they did not in fact appear until after her death: once more, the judgement of her advisors will have deemed them unsuitable to appear in the name of an aristocratic lady as yet unknown to a public quick to raise objections on grounds of taste.

However, given that these two ballads belong very much to the earliest period of her writing in the genre, they need to be placed here, demonstrating further the remarkable range of her interest and her versatility. Unlike one another, they are also a complete departure from the courtly coy 'Chariot of Venus' and the solemn 'Count of Thal'.

One needs to search hard in the *Rosenöl* for the exact source of the material, but there can be no doubt that it was there that she found her inspiration for 'The Fall of the Barmecides' and 'Bajazet' and created two very individual ballads.

'The Fall of the Barmecides' has its source in the account relayed in the *Rosenöl* of the perilous passion between Dschafer, favourite of the Caliph, and the Caliph's sister, Maimuna. From its opening, the poem is full of sensuality: the perfume of the blood orange, the lust and beauty evoked in the first strophe, yet swiftly accompanied by the warning of the second, third and fourth strophes. The darkness and threat are there, to be fulfilled in the terrible image of the closing lines. The reckless love of the couple will lead, as we know from the start, to disaster, not just for the lovers but for the whole race of the Barmecides, condemned to exile and sorrow.

Droste-Hülshoff allows her poem to fall into two contrasting tempos: the quick, dancing movement of the first half, with the woman slipping into the garments of a dancer, as the story related, to lure the mighty Barmecide, but then the account of the ill-fated love which will prompt revenge and hatred from his master and lead to his pathetic execution, strung up and left to the vultures and the spiders at the gates of Baghdad.

The rhythm of the lines and the occasional variation in the length of the strophes express the movement, first of the exuberant young woman as she assumes the role of seductive dancer, but then the aimless wandering of the race of the Barmecides, condemned to a life of shame. This is very much the technique of the ballad, together with the frequent repetitions. It is not surprising that Droste-Hülshoff uses such formal means to tell her story, only that she is already so much in command of them. The final lines deliver a shock in their stark simplicity: the colour and vitality of the poem fade with this image of what is left.

The companion poem tells a different story, and tells it at a different pace, but here, too, she expresses, as she will again and again in her future writings, the contrasts in human fortunes. Bajazet is brought low by circumstances, and betrayed by one he believed to be his friend. He cannot redress his own fate, but his anger and desire for revenge are expressed in his curse of his faithless underling.

This time the ballad quality is above all in the refrain "Oh, sun, conceal your rays!" which runs through the poem as predictably as the fate of the two men. Once more, Droste-Hülshoff shows herself to be familiar with the traditions and brilliant at using them in her inimitable way, very controlled and wonderfully in command of her art. What makes her narrative poetry, like all her work, so remarkable, is her very choice of subject, and the way she uses familiar techniques in her distinctive manner, and with a flourish all her own.

The Fall of the Barmecides

Hand me the blood orange
with the sweet and magical perfume,
the one which has stolen its nourishment
from the loveliest lips.

Did I not say it, oh Maimuna,
kneeling, wringing hands, beseeching,
did I not say it to you seven times over,
not just a thousand times?

"Abandon this love, oh Princess,
abandon this dark love
which burns your whole breast,
bringing you misfortune and danger!

Let not the Caliph come to know of it,
your brother so easily roused to anger,
let not Dschafer, your mighty Barmecide,
bring you to grief,
let Dschafer not bring you to grief,
or you yourself, either, Princess."

Yet what use is wise talk
to the heart enflamed with love?
Only like the whimpering of a little child
in the battle consumed with the fire of rage,
only like a gentle drop of mist
in the flaming building,
only like a light, swaying from the shore
into the dark ocean.

The limbs of the Princess
slip into the garments of the dancer,
and silk floats about her shoulders,
and the zither rests upon her arm.

Ah, how she twists and turns her arms,
lifting the tambourine up high!
Ah, how her footsteps rocked from side to side,
her limbs blooming with passion

so that the Barmecide, glowing,
covers his eyes!

Seven years have vanished,
seven blissful years,
and then, in addition to the seven, three, then five,
and the host of the Barmecides
wander aimlessly in the mountains.

Mothers on the dromedaries,
their lovely eyes blind with weeping,
in their arms the little children,
whimpering into the endless night.

Above the gate of Baghdad,
encircling the skull of Dschafer,
a vulture hurtles up and hurtles over,
and has found no more sustenance
than in the hollow of his eyes
two tiny little spiders still.

Bajazet

The lion and the leopard
were having a singing match.
Pillars of fire start the race,
and the samum[1] is their herald.
Oh, sun, conceal your rays!

What is that slinking there through the yellow sand?

Is it a magic jackal?
Or is it perhaps a large bird,
a badly wounded ibis?
Oh, sun, conceal your rays!

It is no magic jackal,
no badly wounded bird.
It is the mighty Bajazet,
the richest man in Cairo,
he who has thirteen sailing ships,
ships laden with riches.
Upon his shoulders lies the stole,
in his right hand is the staff.
Oh, sun, conceal your rays!

"Woe to you, cursed gold,
you treacherous silver!
And woe to you, Hasse, false friend,
you disloyal servant.
In the night you stole the tents from me,
and took my camels from me."
Oh, sun, conceal your rays!

"You left me like a corpse,
a dried-up mummy,
like an emaciated camel,
like a beast of the desert.
And yet I gave to you great riches,
twenty thousand coris."
Oh, sun, conceal your rays!

"And so I curse you seven times over,
and I damn you one thousand times.
May the sea swallow you up,
and may your burning house bring death to you.
May the lion break your limbs,
the tiger lick your blood,
the beduin rob you,
and the desert be your downfall,
so that you perish in the sand,
gasping, helpless, lost."
Oh, sun, conceal your rays!

[1]Samum: a scorching wind associated with the desert and stirring up dust

CHAPTER IV

❀

THE JEW'S BEECH, AND HER WESTPHALIAN ROOTS: 'THE BOY ON THE MOOR', 'THE SLEEPWALKER', 'THE CASTLE ELF', 'THE GREY MAN'

Although the 1838 volume of some of Annette von Droste-Hülshoff's earlier work could not be deemed a success - for that it was too slight and the selection too random - she seems to have been surprisingly undeterred. On the contrary, the years which followed saw her more than ever full of creative energy and convinced of her 'calling'. These were, after all, years in which she immersed herself in completing and publishing *The Jew's Beech* and producing, as the decade went on, the extraordinary wealth of lyric poetry which continued to appear until shortly before her death in 1848. At the same time, she was delving into the history and essence of her native Westphalia, and this too fed into the poetry and prose of this fruitful period.

The young woman who had grown up knowing the literature of her great German predecessors and nearer contemporaries was also very much at home in the anecdotes and superstitions handed down to her by neighbours and relatives and, perhaps most significantly of all, by her faithful friend, originally her wet-nurse from the village, Marie Kathrin Plettendorf. Thus many of her poems of the 1840s, both lyric and narrative, are redolent with her love and understanding of what was all around her, the countryside itself and the thinking and feeling which imbued it, and with which she felt, to the end of her life, the closest kinship.

This sense of closeness with the region of her birth did not, however, preclude criticism of some of the attitudes and activities of its inhabitants, and nowhere is this more evident than in *The Jew's Beech,* the *Novelle* which some see as central to her work and which certainly has some important links with the ballad poetry under consideration in this volume. This fine prose work occupied her for several years and evolved at a time when she was producing a great deal of other material, both poetry and prose, and demonstrating her range and versatility. This is not the place for a detailed examination of a work which is familiar to readers of German and, through the many excellent translations, readily available in English. It has also been the subject of much critical analysis and lends itself to discussion of its content and style. What follows here, then, is intended to highlight those features which link it to Droste-Hülshoff's narrative poems, and place it in the context of her whole oeuvre.

* * *

The first time Droste-Hülshoff mentions in writing her interest in the story of Friedrich Mergel is to her friend and associate Wilhelm Junkmann, in a letter of August 1837. Although she mentions it only very briefly, together with several other ideas on which she is currently working, it is clear that the story holds a fascination for her since she first heard it, almost certainly in the home of her relatives on her mother's side, the Haxthausens. It was, in fact, her great-grandfather, Caspar Moritz von Haxthausen, who had looked into the case of a young man called Hermann Winkelhannes accused of the murder of a Jewish merchant against whom he was known to have a grudge. Winkelhannes had, however, evaded justice by fleeing and remaining away from his native region for twenty-five years, returning with an account of the suffering he had endured as a slave in Algeria. Although this experience was deemed to be sufficient for him to escape the consequences of his action, his own conscience prevailed and he hanged himself on the tree where the murder had been committed and where the Jews of the neighbourhood had carved a prophesy that the murderer would not be permitted by God to die a natural death.

This was the essence of the strange story that Droste-Hülshoff found when, as a young girl visiting her relatives, she was able to read her uncle August von Haxthausen's version published in the periodical *Die Wünschelrute* in 1818. With its ingredients of a hideous local crime, the flight from justice and the long absence, the simmering desire for revenge in the neighbourhood, and the ultimately inescapable impact of a guilty conscience, it almost certainly remained in her mind during the many years when she was busy with a wide variety of creative work and an emotionally turbulent personal life. As was her custom, she seems to have allowed it to rest until the time was right for her to bring an idea to life, to use the existing bare bones of a story, mould it with her fertile imagination and powerful poetic skill, and in the process produce one of the masterpieces of German narrative literature.

The landscape of Westphalia pervades her narrative, with its brooding darkness and constant sense of threat, as does the often dubious morality of its inhabitants, of which, for all her love of her homeland, she was very much aware. Central to the events are the broad expanses of forest which were constantly threatened by bands of thieves who desecrated it for gain and were in constant conflict with the wealthy landowners, including her own family. Against this background a range of individuals emerge, drawn with her acute insight and contributing, each in his own way, to the tragic course of events. Central to the early stages of the narrative and crucial to the way it develops is the wretched Margreth, Friedrich Mergel's mother, widowed by the inevitable early death of her brutal, drunken husband. Left to bring up her only child, she tries to instil into the boy some of her own simple morality but finds a desperate solution when she is persuaded by her brother to allow him to take a substantial part in his upbringing and, in effect, make him his heir. It is this which proves decisive for the development of Friedrich and leads to his first encounter with another very significant character, the mysterious Johannes Niemand ("Nobody"). Who exactly he is (a neglected servant of the ruthless, conniving uncle? a disowned illegitimate son?) remains unexplained, but, in Droste-Hülshoff's reconception of the historical account, he plays a role of the utmost importance. From the moment Margreth sets eyes on Johannes and actually mistakes him for her son, the reader is confronted not only with the mystery which is a central element of her work and contributes to the ambiguity of its ending, but with one of its most important ingredients. She employs the motif of the *Doppelgänger* , a favourite of her Romantic predecessors and used so strikingly by herself in 'The Fräulein of Rodenschild', to express the chilling duality in Friedrich Mergel and the many contradictions which encircle the pair, throwing up numerous questions and leaving so much unexplained. Only the chance discovery of the scar on the corpse of Mergel provides public exoneration for Johannes and leads to the declaration of the magistrate Herr von S "It is not right that the innocent should suffer for the guilty", but by then Friedrich has paid the price for an action which, even now, is not unambiguously attributed to him. If, when he returns to his homeland after so many years of exile and suffering, he is wishing to repent of a deed he may or may not have committed, then why does Droste-Hülshoff allow him to learn that, in accordance with what she had read in her uncle's account, suspicion had meanwhile fallen on a quite separate person who had actually confessed to the murder all those years before? Is this an indictment of the judicial system, or an accusation of the power of prejudice in a small, interbred community? Is there any kind of message here, from a woman not given to preaching or herself to passing judgement? All these questions surface at the end of a work which taxes the reader and, like several of her ballad poems, supplies no final comment.

A terrible fact remains, however one answers the questions posed: the beech-tree central to the work, bears the tantalizing inscription carved on it by the victim's fellow Jews and only now translated. It warns that whoever approaches this spot will endure the suffering he himself inflicted on another, and the body of Friedrich, who had hoped to find redemption and be permitted Christian burial, is assigned to the knacker's yard. The aristocratic lady of Hülshoff, who must have been adept at looking reality in the face and confronting harsh issues, does not flinch from unpalatable details and even, like the master of mystery she proves herself to be, from throwing a final question into the intriguing mixture. Only later, towards the end of her life, does she appear to offer some kind of redress, when the tragic figure at the heart of 'The Familiar Spirit of the Horse-Dealer' finds the redemption he seeks, not in vengeful payment of his debt to society and to God but through the gentle hand of the Child in the arms of the Madonna.

Droste-Hülshoff had hitherto attempted narrative writing and dramas destined to remain uncompleted, alongside her growing corpus of poetry and particularly at this time struggling to complete her cycle of religious poems, but in this extraordinarily compact narrative she demonstrates a different skill. As was her custom, she worked on it for a long time after its inception, and only in 1842 did it finally appear in print, in instalments published by the prominent publishing firm of Cotta. Its impact was considerable and contributed to her growing reputation. In the context of this volume, it is obviously important, reflecting another aspect of her versatility and demonstrating, as her ballad poems do, her brilliance as a teller of tales. With its complex series of events and the ever-present evocation of the Westphalian region she knew so well, it provides another, different, key to her personality and her creative strengths. Discussion of its genre is irrelevant here, as irrelevant as the investigation of whether the poems one calls loosely 'ballads', or covers with descriptions like 'balladesque' and 'ballad-like', fit in with any preconception of what these terms entail. What matters is that they contribute a further ingredient to the whole and raise, tantalisingly as ever, the question of where her path might have taken her.

* * *

Two poems belong to this time, 'The Boy on the Moor' and 'The Sleepwalker', and although, as so often, one may struggle to call them strictly speaking 'ballads', they need to be included here because they are so much in tune with her developing art.

As a matter of fact, 'The Boy in the Moor' was included by Droste-Hülshoff herself in a specific group and never actually called a ballad, although critics have frequently pointed to its ballad-like qualities. It belongs to an important group of her poems designated 'Images of the Heathland', and when she came to order them for publication in 1844, she was unsure whether this poem should be placed first or last in the group. This suggests it was important to her, and in the present selection, it merits its place at this point. It combines vivid natural description with narrative, as it tells of the walk of the young boy, presumably on his way home from his lessons, across the moor, and the fear and sense of threat it inspires in him.

The atmosphere is created and maintained by the means that Droste-Hülshoff masters in all her writing, both poetry and prose. The sounds and movements all around the young boy are powerfully evoked: the swirling and twirling of the mist, the hissing and whistling and rustling all about him which contribute to his sense of danger lurking and adding to his growing panic, before it all subsides as he comes within sight of the comfort of his home. This is an experience which will remain with him for a long time to come, and one knows that he has been close to alien features of a familiar landscape transformed in the dusk. Not for nothing does she speak of him standing on the threshold, for he will never be quite the same again: he has moved from one stage of his young life to another, and this next stage holds terrors for him which cannot be forgotten.

The moor is peopled by figures conjured up in his mind, from tales heard and superstitions held in his homeland, which is Droste-Hülshoff's homeland too. She will have known of the reputation of the ditcher-lad, of the wretched Lenor spinning away in the reeds, and otherwise ordinary sounds of the landscape about him can be converted easily into the violin-playing of Knauf and the cries of the doomed Margret. Her own knowledge of the neighbourhood of her childhood, and her proximity to it, with all its strange tales and frightening anecdotes, echo in this account of a harmless walk undertaken by one small boy. The result is a powerful poem which remains one of the most famous of Droste-Hülshoff's poems, known by generations right up to the present day who may not be familiar with most of her work.

If one looks at its language analytically, one finds many features which recur again and again and constitute an important aspect of her achievement throughout her life, and in both her poetry and her prose-writing. In translation one can but hope to emulate these features to some extent, and to capture some of the onomatopoeic effects. That said, however, one can render an important aspect of her writing, starting with this poem but continuing on many occasions: the power of her imagination to change the familiar into the unfamiliar and the strange.

The movement of the lines reflects the pace of the boy as he walks, or sometimes rather runs, across the moor. The repetition of the line 'Oh it's frightening walking across the moor' twice in the opening strophe, but then concluding the poem, underlines the intense emotion of this experience, as does the questioning tone -'What's that rustling sound over there by the hedge?' - and the frequent exclamations. There is nothing of the conventional ballad here, but then Droste-Hülshoff is rarely conventional, even when she employs features borrowed from elsewhere and moulds them to her purpose.

The Boy on the Moor

Oh, it's frightening walking across the moor
when the mist of the heath is swirling around,
when the vapours are twirling like phantoms
and hooking their tendrils on to the bushes;
when a little spring spurts up at every step
and there's hissing and singing from every crevice.
Oh, it's frightening walking across the moor
when the clumps of reed crackle in the breeze!

The trembling child is clutching his schoolbook
and running as though someone were chasing him.
The wind is whistling hollowly across the plain -
What's that rustling sound over there by the hedge?
It's the spooky ditcher-lad who squanders his master's
best peat with his drinking.
Hah, hah! the snorting sounds like a mad cow!
The little boy cowers down in terror.

Tree stumps stare out from the bank;
the pine tree nods eerily.

The boy is running, his ears alert,
through giant reeds like spears.
And what trickling and crackling inside!
That is the wretched spinner-woman,
that is the banished spinning Lenor,
who's turning the bobbin in the reeds.

Keep going, keep going! Just keep running!
Onwards, as if someone were trying to catch him!
There's bubbling up in front of his feet,
There's a whistling sound under his soles,
like a ghostly melody.
That's the faithless violin player,
that's the thieving fiddler Knauf
who stole the wedding money.

Then the moor cracks, and a sigh goes up
from the gaping hollow.
"Alas, alas!" then damned Margret cries out:
"Ah, ah! My poor soul!"
The boy leaps like a wounded deer,
and if there were not guardian angels close about him
a grave-digger would discover his little white bones
late one night in the smouldering marshland.

Then suddenly the ground becomes firm,
and over there, near the willow-tree,
the lamp is flickering so cosily.
The boy is standing on the threshold:
he lets out a deep breath, and still looks back,

timidly, towards the moor.

Yes, it was terrible in the reeds.

Oh, it was frightening on the heath.

The Sleepwalker

Just as sure-footed but very different in subject matter and tempo is the next poem, 'The Sleepwalker' which was one of a group that she sent to her friend Levin Schücking in a letter dated April 1844, with a view to publication in a periodical he was planning. In the event, it did not appear until after her death, published by Schücking, but in a collection entitled *Last Gifts* ('Letzte Gaben') which appeared in 1866 and contained a selection of her lyric poetry, including some of her very great late poems.

This one stands on its own, however, telling its story in a way which dispenses with traditional ballad features. Like the previous poem, it is set against the background of the moor, inspired undoubtedly by the landscape of her homeland, and more than likely having its source in some tale that circulated there. Whereas in 'The Boy in the Moor' the sights and sounds of the countryside contribute their own strange magic, transforming the familiar into the threatening and the terrifying, what she does here is conjure up the setting in the opening lines, with their simple, factual question - 'Can you see the tiled roof over there in the grove?' - which requires no answer from the listener but is quickly filled in with twilight, the full moon, the moor, and the awareness that something is afoot. That something is a negative something: it is not a good idea to linger in that place, yet what emerges is that expected components of a threatening situation are actually absent. What is there is not a ghostly spectre, nor a robber, but a thoroughly respectable household.

The second and third strophes deliver the facts in the manner of a newspaper report, based on stories handed down whose veracity cannot be confirmed. But then comes the turning-point as the nocturnal activities of the old man are summed up in the 'evil affliction' which assails him. This is the true substance of this powerful poem, and it takes place beneath the full moon and under the watchful gaze of the servant. The old man counts his money, guarding it jealously, but then he makes his way towards the bedroom, and we must recall the tales that circulate of his cruel behaviour towards his wife and child, long dead.

The poem is extraordinarily compact, its movement measured and deliberate: his corrupt and terrible existence stems from a single act of long ago, when he handed a thief over for execution in return for a single taler. His inhuman treatment of his wife and child and his lasting obsession with money have followed, and the sight of the gallows through the window of his own home reminds him of what he has done: the sound he utters is as though someone were attacking his very soul, for he has surrendered his essential being, and, at the last, any retribution must be left with God. The onlooker may see the little blue flame that denotes a spirit at work, but he must at all cost escape the vapour that is emitted, for judgement does not rest with him. The old man has condemned himself to suffering and the opinion of those who speak of him and are even tempted to add their curses is irrelevant: such people must not condemn themselves by condemning him.

Droste-Hülshoff returns again and again in her work, in her

poetry and of course in *The Jew's Beech*, to the theme of God's judgement on the sinner, and here we can see something that will be overturned in her last great narrative poem 'The Familiar Spirit of the Horse-Dealer'. Meanwhile, we are left with a searing depiction of terrible inhumanity, and the price that is paid for it in this world.

The Sleepwalker

Can you see the tiled roof over there in the grove?
Twilight is closing in, let us go quickly.
Soon the full moon will be rising on the edge of the moor
and then it is not a good idea to linger in these parts.
No ghostly apparition is floating up there among the pine-trees.
No robber is lurking in that shed.
It is a bourgeois house, a bourgeois way of life.
An old man lives there, servants live inside.

The master is old, no one knows how old.
He does not choose to disclose it in the parish records.
His wife died many years ago,
A child died, too, but that is ages past.
They say he would not have a doctor come to her,
that he tortured his sick child with poor food,
but what will they not say to condemn people
when there is a mountain of gold?

Once he was poor, lived wretchedly,
in fact more wretchedly than other people.
And then, the story goes, he handed someone

over to the gallows for a taler.
They say the thief was young and wan with hunger,
his mother sick, but who believes all that?
Envy pursues the rich man. Look at those hovels over there!
That is where poverty resides, but their wealth stayed with him.

You can see him busying himself in the church,
and no one should criticise him for his habits,
but since his bodily strength has deserted him,
the old man succumbs to an evil affliction.
Whenever the full moon is shining,
he wraps himself, sleeping, in his shroud
and climbs out of his bed, fanning the little stub of his candle.
A servant follows him, watching where he is going.

Then out of that hut the workman watches
him counting for hours on end at the window,
filing the gold, making marks with his pen,
and all of a sudden making a grab, as though for the throat of a thief.
Then indeed a cry sounds out,
as if someone were attacking his very soul,
until his arms sink as though struck down by a storm
and he goes trembling on with his little lamp.

His next walk takes him to the room
where there is a little bed standing next to a bigger one.
Then he rocks the cradle this way and that,
as if he were shaking a bottle of fine wine,
and he pours and pours, as if he might never empty it,
and crams and crams as though he were forcing food into the bedclothes,

and seems to be trying to take hold of a pulse,
bent over, as if he were listening to the wheezing of weak breath.

Next he is standing by the other bed,
seems to be bending over and dribbling medicine in.
He tosses a cover over
and seems to be pulling a screen across.
Then in a flash he has reached the pane of glass,
the window from which in the darkness the gallows can be seen.
The servant leaps; you can hear a muffled whimpering sound.
The window clinks, and the room is dark.

Go quickly, more quickly! Look there at the window.
Look how there is a gentle glow and little trembling sparks.
Now a little blue flame starts up: away, just get away!
It seems to me as if a storm is filling the air all about.
Do not look back! You bold man, do not curse him!
Leave him alone with God and justice.
Do you think any curse could add to his sufferings?
Ah, let the thief on the gallows envy him!

The Castle Elf

If 'The Sleepwalker' was based, as it surely was, on some grim
anecdote circulating in her neighbourhood, 'The Castle Elf',
which dates from just a little earlier (1840), is more evidently
the product of popular superstition. Even the castle at the heart
of the poem, with the moat surrounding it, and its crenellations,
was almost certainly a reality in her early life, the kind of
Wasserburg for which Westphalia was, and still is, famous. When

the child Annette was born in Castle Hülshoff in 1797, the birth was doubtless eagerly awaited, and the local population almost certainly turned to the superstition of the Castle Elf to support the hope that this second child of the Baron would be a son and heir, following the birth of her sister Jenny just a year earlier. The wanderer is perhaps as divided as the adult Annette herself, between traditional religious beliefs - he is, after all, a pilgrim on his journey - and deeply entrenched popular ideas. The legend of the appearance of the Castle Elf when a male child is born at the castle swirls like a 'steaming heathen mist' even as he prays to the Virgin Mary for the lady up at the castle who is known to be close to delivering her child. He may not hold this superstition himself, but he is not prepared to reject it. The sounds he hears all around at this hour - long past midnight - are not threatening this time, but they alert him to events outside his normal thinking. When he hears a distant cry and sees a bluish flame shooting past, confusion sets in. It is typical of Droste-Hülshoff to question whether he sees the vision of a child, or just a glow-worm in the reeds, and whether what look like threads of hair are no more than water-lentils.

Reality cuts through in the last strophe, when a window in the castle is thrown up and a command is given by an unmistakably human voice. All ambiguity is banished now. There is suspense in this poem, too, but it is without the threat of the two previous ones, and it does not link so obviously with the setting, even though from the start the brooding castle is the focus of the real events. The announcement of the arrival of the baby to the Baroness in the closing lines is a cry of relief, and, more than that, of joy because the awaited heir has come. The pilgrim who waits and watches from his vantage point in the reeds is no sinister figure but a benign observer. The movement of the lines tells of a period of eager anticipation, a steady building-up of hope and happiness which explodes in the joyous final lines, when reality sets in and he is the recipient of the news. Thus this third poem belongs with the other two in a way, and it shows the diversity of her themes, and the differing moods she brings to bear on them.

The Castle Elf

The castle lies brooding like a sea-dragon
in the sheen of the moonlit pond,
with its crenellated edging, its mossy battlements
and its slated roof.
The ancient oak-trees stand at a distance,
whispering courteously to the waves,
as a grey guard may choose to stand around
its grey sovereigns.

At the entrance the standard-bearer,
a colossus of stone, brandishes the crusader's banner,
and his horse snorts and cavorts about,
as it has done for centuries,
while beside him his hound, like Tantalus,
has panted its way for centuries,
head lowered, towards the river,
with bits of moss growing out of its parched throat.

Even though it is long past midnight,
the castle is still awake.

Streaks of light pass swiftly through the corridor and the room.
From time to time a little lamp bobs up and down
as it crosses the courtyard.
Then the wanderer kneeling in the reeds
at the edge of the pond listens out.

"Ave Maria, give her strength,
and help her through the night".
This is a pious peasant who has
set off early on his pilgrimage.
He knows well enough what the
shining lights signify for his gracious lady,
and eagerly he lets his rosary
slip through his horny hands.

Yet through his Christian prayer there swirls
many a steaming heathen mist.
Is it true, as the legend has it,
that the elf dives into the pool
whenever the first male heir is born
to the dynasty of the Count?
The peasant does not really believe it,
still less would he deny it.

Shyly he glances upwards - the night is clear,
and not at all ghostly.
Just over there one can count on the pair of poplar-trees
the branches along the trunk.
But hush! Is that not footsteps
in the circle of oak-trees? Children's footsteps?

He listens as the steps fall firm and sharp,
upon the parched ground.

Hush, hush! There comes the sound of rustling
across the slope, as if a hind,
emboldened by the moonlight in the dew,
were grazing cautiously over the meadow.
The peasant stops short - the night is bright.
The leaves are glinting in the hedgerows,
And yet, and yet, he cannot see who it is that the footsteps
are carrying towards him.

Then, with a slow creaking sound,
the heavy gate to his right opens up
and, again with a slow creaking sound,
falls back into the green wall.
The peasant is a devout Christian
and quickly crosses himself:
"And even if you are the devil,
you must give way to me on my pilgrimage,"

Then, whish! He feels a touch, soft as a feather.
Then, whish! There is a rustling in the greenery.
Then whish! Something falls hissing into the pond.
so that the bluish reeds and the rushes glimmer,
and, like a shot cracking, a bluish flame falls to the ground,
at the very moment when a cry from the castle
comes trembling across the pond.

The old man has bent forward.

It seems to him as though, as if through glass,
the body of a child were shimmering there, like phosphorus,
damp and indistinct, like gas extinguishing.
An arm is disappearing, a glinting eye is going out.
Was there a glow-worm in the rushes?
A long thread of hair is floating away.
In the end it seems as if they were water lentils.

The peasant stares, up and down,
now into the pond, now into the night.
And then there is the clink of a window opening over there,
and a loud voice cries out:
"Make haste and get saddled! Ride quickly to the town!
Apply the whip and the spur to the Polack!!
Victoria! The Countess has just given birth
to a son!"

One striking feature of 'The Castle Elf' is Droste-Hülshoff's use
of light: the solid castle reflected in the moonlit pond constitutes
an impressive opening, but then, as the night goes on, there
come the signs of activity inside, conveyed in the lamp bobbing
up and down, and cutting across these signs of human life the
crucial moment when the bluish flame brings the message of the
awaited birth. This is a supernatural light, the prelude to the
vision the old man has of the shimmering body of a child, but
the moment passes.

The juxtaposition of the real - the solid evidence of a long-
established dynasty represented in the castle itself and focused
on the stone statue at the portico - and the fleeting supernatural
event which is the heart of the anecdote give another ambiguity

to the poem. However, there is no lingering anxiety, no question left hanging in the mind of the reader, as there is in many of her other poems. On the contrary, the announcement at the end speaks rather of security: the continuity of the dynasty is assured, traditions are upheld and fleeting superstitions rendered immaterial.

The Grey Man

This poem was a product of the same year, and like 'The Castle Elf', it has its source in Droste-Hülshoff's Westphalian homeland. It is not a superstition this time, however, but possibly an anecdote known to her and her kinsfolk, a strange tale of unexplained happenings in a little castle in the forest. This time it is not an ancestral home with its inhabitants anxious about the continuity of the line that lies at the heart of the poem. The castle has been converted into a paper mill by its owner, who appears to have more ambition than actual business acumen, a small detail that remains unelaborated on but is typical of Droste-Hülshoff's keen interest in her fellow human beings. The people assembled there on this wet and windy autumn evening are merchants from diverse places, a motley bunch it would appear, who enjoy a noisy evening together before falling into inebriated sleep when their host decides it is time for bed. We learn little about them as individuals, beyond the displeasure of Van Neelen at the weather, which does not commend itself to a stay in the country, and the fact that Waller is blond, a detail that will remain with us as the events of the night proceed. It is upon him that the rest of the poem concentrates, beginning with the detail that he remembers to take with him to bed his copy of *Ivanhoe*. That he shares with so many in nineteenth-century Europe a liking for Walter Scott is unsurprising, of course, but it prepares the way for the ending of the story and the questions that remain.

Deeply immersed in his reading, Waller is oblivious to the candle burning down and creating a pool of wax: he hardly notices the noises all about him, but appears to be absorbing them into the story he is reading. However, he cannot ignore the sound of the window bursting open, and his illusions are dispelled and replaced by the reality of the room he is in. A certain gentle humour characterises this poem, sombre though it may seem to be in its strange outcome: the ancestral portraits that line the walls seem to be passing comment on the unlikely guest, and he in turn responds with mockery as he prepares to sleep. In that sleep there are two ingredients, of course: drink, and the influence of the novel he has just been reading with such enthusiasm. Small wonder that he converts the mists that swirl through the room into a phantom dressed in grey and threatening him, while his response is to fire the pistol with which he has seen fit to arm himself for the night. The part of his brain which is still alert knows that to fire a second time would be absurd, and yet another shot rings out. Whatever happens or does not happen now is vividly conveyed and constitutes the terrifying core of this nocturnal episode.

When Waller is discovered the next morning stretched out cold, we cannot be sure whether he is alive or dead, until we are told that he is revived from what turns out to be a swoon. 'He was not deranged' as we might conclude, but he is anxious, clearly having a recollection of what had come to pass and concerned that the corpse he recalls in his bed the night before should not lead to the uncovering of a dreadful deed. All is well, however: no one has heard anything, and his fellow guests dismiss it as a nightmare. But perhaps they are not so sure: they make their departure very swiftly, and Droste-Hülshoff's comment 'They were all much too clever and altogether too educated' begs several questions.

Once more, she leaves us with a telling final line: the blond hair of Waller has turned ice-grey and, once more, we are left to draw our own conclusions.

The Grey Man

The little castle stands in the forest,
fashioned from raw ashlar,
with crenellations and little windows
through which the guns once protruded.
On the pond the tall reeds rustle.
The bridge sways and creaks in the gale.
And in the middle of the courtyard,
solid, massive as a mortar, stands the tower.

Now you can see ranged around it
many a fiery-red tiled roof,
and as the press rises and falls,
the steam engine lets out a whistle.
The mould emits a cracking sound,
the sheet of paper shrieks,
the nearby saltpetre produces a mist,
and above the grey crest can be read: Moulin à papier.
But the Brussels merchant is hardly pleased about the way

the boiler bubbles up and foams.
Once upon a time he had dreamt the finest dream
about the land and the air around it.
That was just the spot to escape
from the clutches of figures!
Not a big place, and yet quite noble,
and it did not need much staff.

But just one night he made himself
comfortable - or uncomfortable-
in his little castle, and since then he only
fluttered over it like a bird.
Then he glanced up at the windows,
locked up like sacristies,
and probably shrugged his shoulders
with a sigh - or two.

It was around September-time,
when the master of the house
was standing in the hall, his smock damp with rain,
bent over, poking the fire in the hearth,
he and his guests, all in the smoke:
Van Neelen, Redel, Verney, Dahm,
and then blond Waller, too,
who had just arrived from Smyrna.

The wind was puffing in the chimney,
the rain spurting down from the roof,
and when a little flame shot out of the fire,
the room seemed twice as desolate.
The guests were all on hand,

soothing their host's displeasure.
Only Van Neelen was standing by the window,
grumbling about this excursion into the country.

But after a while things got better.
The wind had fanned the flames
and the rain was left outside.
Bottles of champagne were brought,
and there was not much need for candelabras.
It was like a students' celebration:
as soon as a bottle was empty
a candle was pressed into it.

The less there is, the more they laugh.
The wine is hot, the food excellent.
Many a crude little joke is played,
and many a fine story told.
At last, glowing with wine and talk,
the master of the house pushes back his chair.
"I invited you to a country excursion,
but it has turned out to be a water-trip.

However, since the loveliest ship
finds its way to harbour in the end,
good night, my friends,
and take anything you fancy with you."
Thereupon each of them seizes a bottle
with a laugh - doors open and close -
and Waller, just as he is going, slips his
copy of *Ivanhoe* out of his jacket pocket.
It was deep in the night,

and outside the gale was still howling,
puffing and hissing at the window-frame,
and twisting the bell-rope in the tower.
Waller was lying in his bed,
reading his *Ivanhoe* so attentively
that one could think that before daybreak
the kingdom of England would be at peace.

He did not notice that the candle
was burning low in the bottle,
and that the wax was pouring in heavy drops
so that a pool had formed beneath.
As though in a dream he heard
the creaking of the windows, muted by the blind,
and heard the doors jerking on their hinges
and making a rasping sound as they struggled.

He is hugely enjoying the antics of Friar Tuck:
his bow twangs, the glade rustles -
when all of a sudden there is an almighty jolt,
and hui! the window bursts open with a clang.
He started up - the dream was gone! -
and covered the light with his hand.
Ha! how desolate was the room!
A veritable romantic poem!

The armchair feudal gold,
the griffin's claw upon the marble table,
and above the mirror rolls forth a banner,
the blue of carpets, fluttering in the draught

which puffs its way through the cracks.
The ancestral portraits are almost alive
and shake their helmeted heads in fury
at the plebeian guest.

Blond Waller enjoyed a little bit of horror himself
and nodded mockingly
towards the noble gentlemen,
as if he were issuing a bold challenge to them
The clock burrs: already one o'clock, indeed!
He stretched himself like a boa,
looked over at the pair of pistols,
and then armed himself for sleep.

He raised the bottle one more time
and lit up the walls: exactly like an old hall
out of a Scottish novel!
And is that mist or smoke swirling
through the cracks in the door,
and whirling in the breath from the draught,
filling the misty panelling?

A thing, a thing! like grey, all dressed in grey,
the shapes are swaying - strange!
Yet, are his eyes getting sharper?
He gradually takes in the shape of the limbs,
how above the iron cudgel the column of smoke is billowing,
black and heavy.
A jerking movement flutters towards him,
and yet it has a human form!

He was a hotheaded fellow when wine
stirred him up.
"Who's there?" and with a crack
 he gently cocked his pistol.
Waller has stretched out his arm:
"Who's there?" - a pause - "Or I shoot!"
And the bullet shot out. He heard it hit against the door
and then drop with great force.

The sound of the shot echoes to the ceiling,
and a heavy layer of mist, the vapour of powder
fills the room.
It moves away, disappears, and now
the spectre is standing in the middle of the room,
just like a grey image in stone,
its outline sharp and unbroken,
its features noble, stern and pure.

A grey beret on grey hair,
with grey plumes in it.
Waller has loaded a second time,
softly and deftly,
but still he hesitates.
If it is a vision it would be ludicrous to shoot,
and if it were a human being - his blood surges within him-
a dandy, who was acting on a dare.......?
Another jolt! And another crack,
and the smoke of a gun. Was that a groan?
He did not hear the sound of a bullet ricocheting.
It's over! It's happened!

Waller starts: "Cursed brain!"
Suddenly he is cold as ice,
and the perspiration of fear is on his brow.
He stares at the encircling mist.

A moan! Or is it the wind?
But no: the splinters of glass are clinking.
Oh, God! Something is fidgeting about - but no!
It is the smoke pushed by the draught
that is floating and wandering around.
It whirls up, wave upon wave, and now,
like a grey stone image, the figure is standing by the bed,
at the point where the curtain drops.

And now there is a crunching sound, like sand,
like a spark alive with electricity.
Now a finger moves, and now a hand,
and now gradually a foot is raised,
high, ever higher. Waller waves,
and then quickly he makes room for it,
and slowly it sinks into the pillows,
like a felled tree.

"Ah! I've got you!" He has caught it
and is clutching its arms as in a trap.
A corpse! Dead stiff and naked!
He falls back with a start, and thereupon
It passes slowly over him, like the millstone,
heavy as lead.

At that Waller let out a cry,
and his senses had departed.

The next morning they found him
stretched out, cold, in his room.
It was only a swoon,
and soon he was woken up to consciousness.
He was not deranged, only anxious,
and asked if anyone had been disturbed.
But they had all slept soundly,
and no one had heard the shot.

Thus it was immediately dismissed as a dream,
and all just as a nightmare.
However, they left the region
and hastened across country.
They were all much too clever,
and altogether too educated.
But from that night on blond Waller
had ice-grey hair.

CHAPTER V

✤

RÜSCHHAUS AND MEERSBURG: BALLADS OF HER MATURE YEARS

Annette von Droste-Hülshoff was born in the Castle of Hülshoff, one of the castles of Westphalia surrounded by a broad moat for which the region is famed. Here she grew up as the second daughter of an ancient Catholic family, headed at that time by her father Clemens August, to whom she was clearly devoted and from whom she derived her enthusiasm for the wonders of the world of nature. Her relationship with her mother, though always loyal and correct, was more formal and more restricted, and, since Therese von Droste-Hülshoff assumed the control of what might be termed her education, this was somewhat uninspiring. However, the highly intelligent Annette absorbed the influences that abounded in an educated household, where she was exposed to literature and art and music, in all of which she showed distinct talent. It was a busy home, in which friends and relatives came and went. Annette benefited from social connections which meant that, in spite of the awkwardness that was sometimes remarked upon, she was able to develop an assurance perhaps beyond her years and in general command respect from a social circle outside her immediate family. Only to her closest associates and sometimes in her later writings does she betray the doubts and insecurities which obsessed her even in her youth and account for the duality and contradictions underlying her life and much of her work.

Her first emotionally devastating experience came in the summer of 1820, when she became embroiled in a friendship with two young men. Given her nature and her lack of experience and possibly of guidance, she mishandled a situation which was probably always destined to get out of hand. However, its impact left a mark seemingly out of proportion to the actual course of events, as far as posterity can interpret them. What is so often described as the 'catastrophe' of her youth, remained with her and governed much of the rest of her life. That is not to say that she did not function effectively in human relationships on a certain level: she was sociable, loving and warm-hearted, but in her own estimation it looks as though she remained scarred. If one links with this the increasing physical frailty which undoubtedly contributed to a relatively early death, it is possible to see her as a tragic figure, though the stature of her work and her extraordinary versatility lead ultimately to a rejection of this view. She is a woman of courage and vigour, and her voice rings out loud and clear, and unmistakably her own.

Her early efforts in writing, poetry and prose, drama and narrative, and not least her personal letters, are interesting and often quite original, even though she discarded some of them and left a number of tantalizing fragments. However, it was not until what was to be the last decade of her short life that she truly found that voice and began to establish some kind of reputation. By 1838, several circumstances had come together. Her father had died in 1826, leaving her not only with her grief at the loss of her treasured parent, but with an abrupt change in the domestic position of the Hülshoff family. Her elder brother and his wife took over at the ancestral castle, and she and her mother and only sister moved to the much more modest house which was to be her home from then on. From the somewhat claustrophobic Rüschhaus in the depths of the country some distance from Münster, she began to travel, not widely, but nevertheless away from home, visiting relatives in the Rhineland and building on friendships established on an earlier brief visit to Cologne and Bonn which had been cut short by the family bereavement. The acquisition of new relationships led to a widening of her experience and a consequential broadening in her writing, with two more ambitious projects, large-scale epic poems 'The Hospice on the Great St Bernhard Pass' and 'The Doctor's Legacy'.

Again, family changes intervened: the death of her much-loved younger brother Ferdinand, the marriage of her sister Jenny to the distinguished Count Josef von Lassberg and their departure to Switzerland. Typically, however, these losses, and even her own recurrent illnesses, in which depression played a major role, led not, as they might have done at an earlier stage of her career, to a diminution of her creative energy but to an upsurge in it. Her mother was frequently absent visiting Jenny in Switzerland and Annette was often alone in the rather isolated house with her friend and confidante, originally her wet-nurse from the village, Maria Kathrin Plettendorf. Although she busied herself with conscientious attention to neighbours and distant relatives in need of company from time to time, her main concentration was now on her writing, though her letters refer, mostly without complaint, to frequent such distractions.

Her commitment to her work culminated in the slight and frankly not very successful volume of poems published in 1838. This was, for all its limitations, something of an achievement, published semi-anonymously because of the restrictions on a lady of her class and a totally unknown one at that, but the circumstances of its appearance were not propitious. The publisher was a small local firm, Aschendorff, not destined to advance her reputation, and the devoted friends who supported her, the blind professor of philosophy, Christoph Bernhard Schlüter, and the aspirant poet Wilhelm Junkmann, lacked the knowledge and worldly wisdom to harness their admiration for her work to her advantage. The volume can be read today in a rather charming reprint, which shows it to be a somewhat random selection poorly arranged, and unsurprisingly it received very little attention, still less acclaim. It was a start, however, and it seems to have precipitated her into a new literary environment and a period of new enthusiasm and confidence.

In the literary society which had recently been formed in Münster, and very much among friends, her work was appreciated, and she began to be taken seriously by people who valued literature and sought to further it. Even the year which she spent with her sister and her brother-in-law and her ill-disguised dislike of Switzerland did not distract her seriously from her work and her new-found sense of purpose, and by the time she returned to the Rüschhaus, clearly glad to be back where she felt she belonged, she had produced some poems which owe their existence to the landscape around Eppishausen, and the very different beauty of the Alps. Ironically, the cycle of poems 'Der Säntis' represents a complete departure for her, and a real taste of things to come. Not least, it was at this time that she returned to her work on 'The Spiritual Year', which she had abandoned almost twenty years earlier in her despair at the events of her 'catastrophe year'. This is a Droste-Hülshoff with a new vitality and a real conviction of her purpose and her ability to achieve it. It is at this time that she begins to combine the writing of ballads with the pure lyric poems on which her attention, and arguably her fame, will now rest, and it is at this time, too, and in the context of the Münster literary circle, that a new name enters her story.

She had last met Levin Schücking, the son of her friend Katharina (née Busch), six years earlier, when he had come to visit her at the Rüschhaus following the death of his mother. Schücking's 'Lebensbild' ('Picture of a Life'), published fourteen years after her death, contains some of the most significant details of the nature and life of the poet, and of their acquaintance which stemmed from this early encounter between the devastated teenage boy and the woman now in early middle age. It is clear that she made an impression on him, not only through her striking physical appearance - the bright blue eyes and the mass of fair hair - but through her obvious genuine concern for the vulnerable boy, with whom she must have shared the bond of the bereaved. If he did not follow up her invitation to return to see her, this was almost certainly due to his own emotional turmoil and the demands of the studies on which he was now embarking. What emerges from his account is her kindness and the awe he felt in the presence of a woman who, while as yet not famous, was clearly acutely intelligent and fascinating in the range of her interests and her concern for his well-being. He notes, probably with hindsight, that she appeared to feel somewhat guilty that her friendship with his mother had not been as close as Katharina might have wished and that she seemed to see the opportunity to redress this lack now in her dealings with the orphaned boy, whose father had disappeared from the family picture and who was now virtually alone in the world. This is the kind of observation one can value in Levin Schücking, who, as things turned out, did not always treat Annette with the same concern, but to whom we owe the first major edition of her works, and this very percipient picture of her as a person.

Posterity can speculate on the nature of the relationship between these two people, and indeed posterity has done so, but what matters most is the regard he sincerely had for her, and his profound understanding of her genius. It was Schücking who, by his own account hardly to be disputed, told her that her true genius lay in the realm of the lyric, and to this one could add that her achievement in the ballad genre lies not least in her capacity to instil into the ballad the essence of the lyric. Schücking's early studies were in law, but he subsequently established a reputation as a journalist and critic. He was certainly not first and foremost a poet, and Droste-Hülshoff observed, with characteristic candour, that it surprised her that he was not a better poet, considering that he was such an excellent judge of poetry. How one sees the personal relationship between them is more complex and perhaps impossible to ascertain with the evidence available. Far more important is the importance she attached to it and to the role he played in her development as a poet. That should perhaps be enough: if this was a love affair, it was so possibly only within her understanding of love. What is evident from what she wrote about the brief time they spent together, at first in Münster and then when he joined her in Meersburg, where, at her instigation, he was engaged as librarian to her brother-in-law, is that it was extremely intense, intense enough to support and encourage her as she rose to new heights as an artist, and to sustain her afterwards. The letters she wrote to him now betrayed both the devastation she felt at his departure and the sense she had that she could proceed alone.

The ballad poems with which this volume is concerned, like the great lyric period, emerge from these two places and cannot be separated from her friendship with Levin. Although critics, following Clemens Heselhaus, speak of the 'Rüschhaus ballads' and the 'Meersburg ballads', there is really no distinction such as this seems to imply. In the years which followed the renewal of her acquaintance with Levin Schücking, she moved between Westphalia and the very south of Germany, where, on the shore of Lake Constance, she stayed with Jenny and her family, and even bought, with the first major income from her writing, the little house - the *Fürstenhäusle* - in the vineyards high above the Lake which is today a moving destination for those who seek her out on a pilgrimage. That she died not there but within the austere walls of Meersburg Castle, faithfully cared for by her loving sister, her devoted brother-in-law and the little twin nieces to whom she was herself so devoted, is part of the sadness one senses in this woman. Her grave is not where she hoped it would be, in the dark woods of Westphalia, but in the little churchyard in Meersburg, but her heart may never have left her homeland.

The poems she wrote in this enormously productive period bridge the two very different places with such very different landscapes hundreds of miles apart in Germany. The voice is not different, and the inspiration to that brilliant voice which moves between lyricism and dark narrative is the figure of Levin Schücking. For all his perceived flaws - his ambition, his thoughtlessness and even the betrayal she felt he had inflicted on her (see p. 195 below) - he recognized the remarkable nature of her genius and eventually devoted the latter part of his life to conserving it.

The Fräulein of Rodenschild

Droste-Hülshoff wrote 'Das Fräulein von Rodenschild' in the late autumn of 1840 and sent it to Levin Schücking in response to his request for some ghost stories for the illustrated collection of writings on the countryside and customs of Westphalia which he was producing in collaboration with his friend Ferdinand Freiligrath. In the event, Droste-Hülshoff made a substantial contribution to this volume (*Das malerische und romantische Westfalen*) which appeared in 1841, although, as was the fate of so much of her work at this time, it remained anonymous. However, there is no mistaking the features which distinguish this poem, like the others which she sent to Schücking for inclusion in the work, as the product of her hand, and of this brief period of her life which is marked by an extraordinary flowering of her poetry. Nor can one fail to see in the ballads of these two or three years her increasing mastery of this genre, side by side with that of pure lyric poetry, and, of course, of prose narrative, exemplified above all in *The Jew's Beech*. In the artistic development which culminated in the abundant creativity of these very few years, the ballads occupy an important place. With time not on her side as she moved towards increasing frailty and her early death, Annette von Droste-Hülshoff managed to muster the strength to secure her place in the German literature of the 19ᵗʰ Century, and in European literature of all time.

One of the most remarkable - and fascinating - features of her narrative poems is the variety of subject matter to which she was drawn, as she made her way from a poem like 'Emma and Edgar', with its echoes of the ballads she had read as a child, to her powerful retelling and rethinking of familiar motifs which proclaim her originality and her genius.

In 'The Fräulein of Rodenschild' she uses a central motif of Romantic literature, that of the double, the *Doppelgänger*, and endows it with a quality which chills and thrills and ensures that this is among the most memorable of her narrative poems. Although the explanation which accompanies it in the Westphalia book where it made its first appearance points to the origin in a legend about happenings at the castle of the Count of Rietberg, subsequent evidence from Levin Schücking and Annette herself suggests that the inspiration was much closer to home.

In his *Lebensbild*, Levin recounts an experience told to him by Annette, and it corresponds very closely to the events in the poem and argues strongly for its autobiographical nature. She had told him, he writes, that, asleep in her father's house in the night leading to the dawn of Easter Day, she had been woken by the sound of the household singing to greet the sacred day and, listening from an upstairs window, had observed the assembly below, just as the Fräulein in the poem does, until her attention was alerted to a figure emerging, with long blond hair and with a candle in her hand, and moving slowly down the staircase. The servants, she told him, had made way for the figure as it passed by them and disappeared into the darkness. She had herself then returned to her bed and to her sleep. On the following morning, she had asked the first servant she met about the nocturnal singing and received the simple response that yes, they had been singing and that she herself had joined them: indeed, they had been worried that their mistress might catch cold. She had not pursued the conversation but had obviously retained the events in her memory for their reappearance in this poem.

That Annette von Droste-Hülshoff was susceptible to psychic experiences is attested in her own writings from her early youth, and from the comments of those who knew her well and in whom she dared to confide her awareness that she shared with so many of her country-folk this closeness to the supernatural and to matters explicitly forbidden by her Catholic faith. Rather like the old pilgrim in 'The Castle Elf', she almost certainly found herself torn between conventional religious beliefs and superstition. However, if in her younger days she was reluctant to admit to this, the content of many of her greatest poems, and particularly of her ballads, reveals someone who came to terms with this dilemma and absorbed it into her understanding of herself.

A letter to her mother as late as January 1842 contains evidence of her obsession with tales of ghostly apparitions, and even of her delight in them. One experience related to her was of the regular appearance to the master and mistress of a castle known to be haunted of their doubles. These apparitions could be encountered in the ancient corridors while the couple were sitting quietly in their living-room, reading and knitting. 'Isn't that lovely?' she asks her mother ('Ist das nicht schön?'), suggesting that Annette had long since accepted such things as a normal part of her life and one which she could use unquestioningly in her work. Her friends the Kessel family, of whom she writes quite openly in this same letter to her somewhat straitlaced and tight-lipped mother, could tell tales which made one's hair stand on end. Undoubtedly this was an aspect of her personality and essential make-up which her devoted mother and her much more down-to-earth sister Jenny accepted, along with all the other features which they neither shared nor entirely understood.

When her close friend Adèle Schopenhauer wrote to her in response to her reading of 'The Fräulein of Rodenschild', she professed to having liked the poem but found the ending unconvincing: how could the young woman have gone on living her life and dancing away at balls in the castle after such an experience? (Letter dated 27 June 1841). Intelligent and in general appreciative as Adèle was, she must have failed to recognize that it was possible to live a life on two levels, as Annette did, and to bear the ice-cold hand of the Fräulein or the grey hair of Waller as the tangible signs of a powerful psychic experience. 'The Fräulein of Rodenschild' perhaps tells us as much about the complex inner life of Annette von Droste-Hülshoff as all the thousands of pages of her letters.

The autobiographical content of this ballad apart, it is of very great interest and conveys much evidence of the skill of Droste-Hülshoff in conveying tension and the atmosphere of time and place. This skill is evident in her lyric poetry but, in this period when she produced her outstanding narrative poems too, it consistently forms the backbone of the tales she tells with such pungency and originality. The way is opening to a climax in 'The

Familiar Spirit of the Horse-Dealer' which horrifies with its stark presentation of supernatural events, yet ends with a gentle message of forgiveness and compassion.

Compared with some of her other ballad-type poems of the early 1840s, 'The Fräulein of Rodenschild' is strangely simple. The immediacy of the two questions in the first two lines sets the scene, yet suggests that something is pending. It is too warm for an April night, and the suggestion is that the passion of the young woman at the core of the poem is about to erupt into a significant experience, and a rare one. There is expectation and frustration as she awaits the midnight hour which begins the new and special day, and, when it comes, it is marked by something traditional and familiar: the singing of the assembled household in recognition of the sacred events of Easter Day.

It is against this background of the norm, the familiar and the natural that the central event transpires: the appearance of the *Doppelgänger* watched by the lady herself and witnessed by the ordinary people of the household. Much of the effect of what Droste-Hülshoff relates lies in the details: the young woman gets up from her bed like a hind, smooth and slender; she unlaces her bodice; and she pushes her hair back under her little cap.

As she listens at the window, new sounds join the singing: the cry of the owl and the howling of the wind, and the creaking of the gate. The singers are identified: the familiar members of an aristocratic household, individual servants who behave in their accustomed ways, forming a procession which is only interrupted when suddenly they see something unexpected: the appearance of the lady they recognize as the young mistress of the house, whom the watcher at the window also recognizes - as herself.

The spectre fills her with horror and a sense of madness, as she watches the progress of this double of hers, and sees the rows of people, the ordinary people she knows so well, move to one side to let it pass, just as Annette had apparently related to Schücking. The pace of the poem increases as she desperately tries to pursue this vision, until, in the archive-room to which it has headed, with herself now close behind, she notes its movements and identifies them as her own.

When they stand face to face, we see again, on each of them, the little cap she pulled on before, and then all the focus is on her outstretched hand, matched exactly by the hand of the other figure, with the same ruby on each hand. But now the poet acknowledges the difference: the one is 'the living woman', the other 'the vision'.

Enough has now been seen and said, and the vision vanishes. The action fast forwards, and, with the economy so central to this whole poem, the final strophe encompasses all the relevant information. The Fräulein is a beautiful young girl, wild and happy, capable of dancing at social gatherings, but always concealing her ice-cold hand with a glove, and whatever of that nocturnal episode at Eastertide remains with her is subsumed in the passing comment that she had been ill for a time, but years ago, and that it is the adjective 'crazy' (*toll*) that attaches to her now.

The Fräulein of Rodenschild

Are the April nights so sultry then?
Or is the blood of virgins boiling hot like this?
She closes her eyes, lies so still,

and listens to the pounding flood of her heart.
"Oh, will day never, never come?" she asks.
"Oh, will the hour never, ever strike?
I am awake, and even the clock is resting.

But listen, it strikes: one, two, and three, -
and still goes on? Six, seven and eight,
eleven, twelve. Oh, God, was that a cry?
But no: the sound of singing rises above the
watchtower, and now I understand. With
pious lips the household greets the hour,
the coming of the sacred Easter night."

The Fräulein moves her pillow to one side,
and, like a hind, she rises from her resting-place.
She has unlaced her bodice
and now she pushes her locks into her little cap.
Then softly opening the window, softly,
she listens to the melody as it rises slowly,
accompanied by the whimpering of the owl.

Oh, dark the night, and frightening the wind!
The banners swirl upon the creaking gate.
With hooded lanterns, one by one,
the household proceeds out of the great hall.
The gatekeeper stretches, still half dreaming;
the huntsman tugs at the wick of his candle
as he comes dawdling along, and the Moor is yawning like an ogre.

What's this? How they go hurtling off in all
directions! The men arrange themselves in
rows, and the respectable grey-haired lady's
maid watches over the young girls.
"Did they see me through the gap in the
curtains? No, their eyes are fixed on the
balcony, and now their heads are slowly turning.

Oh, alas for my eyes! Am I mad?
What is that sliding along the banister?
Did I not look like that in the mirror?
Those are my limbs - what a dazzling light!
Now it raises its hands, like bits of fluffy cotton.
That is the way I stroke my brow and my hair.
Alas, am I mad, or is my end nigh?"

The Fräulein turns pale and then grows red.
The Fräulein does not avert her gaze,
and, gently touching the steps, the vision
descends the stone staircase.
In its right hand it carries the lamp,
and the little flame trembles above the ramp,
fading away, blue, like an elf's light.[1]

Now it is floating beneath the vaulting stars,
like sleepwalkers in a dream,
and now the phantom moves through the rows
of people, and each one takes a step to the side.
And now it is gliding across the threshold without a sound,
and now the light is shining again inside,
and it is climbing up the winding staircase.

The Fräulein does not hear the murmuring,
does not see the vacant, timid looks.
Her eyes are firmly fixed upon the bluish light
as it drifts like mist over the tiles.
Now it's in the great hall - now in the archive room.
Now it is standing silently in the depths of the recess
Now more and more faint: ah! it has turned pale!

"You must stop for me! I am going to catch you!"
And like an eel the bold maiden slips her way
through the night, through twists and turns.
Here she almost falls, there her gown catches.
She treads softly, softly. Oh! The senses of spirits
are alert, and the vision must not escape.
Yes, she is brave, I swear she is!

A dark frame, the entrance to the archive-room.
Ah! locks and bolts! She stands in a trance
and gently, hesitatingly, she places first her eye
and then her ear against the edge of the gap in
the door. Pitch black inside - and yet she thinks
she hears the rustle of parchment, and a swift
movement along the wall.

So, battling against the beating of her heart,
she holds her breath. She listens and bends down.
What is that softly dawning by her side?
The light of a glow-worm: it whirls, it mounts up,
and arm upon arm, a step away,
the ghost is leaning against the door
and, like her, bending towards the adjacent slit.

She steps back - the vision too, and then she steps
closer, and the figure does as well
Now the two of them are standing, eye to eye,
boring into one another with a vampire's force.
The same little cap covers their hair,
the same linen, white as snow, falls
casually over the limbs of each of them.

Slowly the Fräulein stretches out her right hand,
and slowly, as in a mirror, the same hand
stretches out, line matching line and wearing the same ruby.
Now there is a movement:
the living woman senses it,
as if a blast of wind were cutting through her.
The vision fades, floats away, and has vanished.

And when there is dancing in the hall,
you can see a girl, beautiful and wild.
She was sick for a time years ago,
and now she always conceals her right hand
in a glove. They say it is cold as ice,
and yet the maiden is happy, and they have always
called her the crazy 'Fräulein of Rodenschild'.

[1)]The bluish light suggests the supernatural at work (See 'The
Sleepwalker' and 'The Castle Elf')

The Cry of the Vulture

'The Cry of the Vulture' contains some ingredients expected of a traditional ballad: a band of robbers waiting to pounce on a carriage in the forest and a lovely young girl making her way through the countryside oblivious to the dangers that may await her. However, nothing about the poetry of Annette von Droste-Hülshoff ever conforms entirely to traditions, although she may borrow from them and use them for her always original purposes. Already a hint is contained in the knowledge we have that she changed the title of this poem before sending it to Levin Schücking for publication, along with a substantial group of ballad-type poems of this same period, around 1840-42. In her draft version she gave it the rather pedantic title that surfaces as its message in the final lines: 'Heaven holds its protection over innocence'. The title she then chose is much more effective: succinct and unambiguous, it links the three separate scenes of the poem and leaves the moral to the very end.

Actually, it is far from apparent that her intention was to point a moral in this poem. She recounts an event in vivid terms. The band of robbers is a motley bunch, it seems, and the opening instructions from the leader to his men identifies them clearly, with particular emphasis on Rieder, the firebrand with his reputation for violent behaviour. Their intention is clear: they are lying in ambush, awaiting the arrival of a coach with its escort of foot-soldiers. Their reputation strikes fear throughout the neighbourhood. They take up their allotted positions, based on the hut which used to be a shelter for the gamekeeper on the estate where there was once a castle, now in ruins.

Having established the scenario without which the poem would not exist, Droste-Hülshoff changes the tempo and concentrates on the forest setting into which the pretty young girl will enter, unaware of impending danger. So briefly and so carefully, she juxtaposes the silence of the forest and its loneliness with the drunken activity inside the hut, and the sound of the bees is contrasted with the sound of the knives of the robbers being prepared for their attack. Her language changes to describe the charm and beauty of the girl, who may belong in these parts but can still find herself lost as she wanders along without an aim.

The connection between the two main characters is, of course, the quarry, where, as we know from the very first strophe, Rieder will already have taken up his assigned post. As she settles herself down, she comes up with the slightly whimsical idea that she is like the image of a saint in a shrine.

Yet we know that the threat is there, and even as she closes her eyes and dozes off, the danger is growing. When the sound comes, we are prepared for it, but the poem does not ever say whether this is the awaited signal that the carriage is on its way, or the cry of the bird of prey she later sees overhead which will indicate the direction she will take as she guides the carriage people to human habitation and safety. That does not matter, any more than it matters that we never find out what the peril she manages to avoid would have been. Annette's close friend Adèle Schopenhauer was evidently much taxed by this ambiguity ('seduction or death?' she asks in a letter of 21 April 1841) but it simply is not important in a poem which succeeds through its subtlety and power to suggest. Adèle herself wrote that she liked the poem, as did those who reviewed it, but, as seems to have been her wont, she often picked on trivial features, possibly to assert her literary equality with her infinitely more gifted friend. She is right, though, when she describes the poem as 'eigentümlich'. It is indeed unusual, and characteristic of one aspect of Droste-Hülshoff's art, with its gentle irony, its close observation of the natural setting and of the people she places in it, her depiction of the potential for a catastrophic outcome, and the ease with which she evades that.

The little conversation between the young girl and the money-dealer sums up the situation. She knows the dangers, but she does not seem to have heeded them herself in her innocent wanderings. Whether the cry of the vulture was real or human is not relevant either, but as Droste-Hülshoff reviews the events that evening, they are swiftly seen from three differing perspectives. It is a charming poem, which undoubtedly merited the appreciation of her critics and, with its lightness of touch, it demonstrates another somewhat unexpected facet of her skill in story-telling.

The Cry of the Vulture

"Quiet now! - you go to the trap!
 You on the left towards the split tree!
And this ruffian can
take up his position on the edge of the cliff.
That way you can look right across the land
and see the coach coming towards you,
and Rieder there, the firebrand,
can post himself in the quarry.

Then keep your eyes and ears alert,
and at the first sound of the wheels,
screech like an owl - and if the vehicle proceeds,
make that sound again. But if danger looms -
go on patrol- and if you see the foot soldiers coming,
let out the call
of the bearded vulture, three times,
as though from the top of the reef.

Now, Rieder, another word to you:
you are rightly known as the firebrand,
but - I beg you - no antics like recently
with your bare hands!"
It is the sergeant speaking, and a stir
passes through the gathering, and a slight buzz,
as they softly shoulder their rifles,
and their knives clink at their belts.

A strange bunch! On the one hand a huge figure
with a hacked-out face,
and on the other a little lad who looks so ladylike -
a dainty thug!
That man over there so gently stroking his tresses
with his glinting blade
peers out of his blue eyes
for all the world like an impoverished troubadour.

It is daylight, but the little band
fears no particular hour - it's all the same to them.
This is the Red Band, notorious far and wide,

feared throughout the realm.
A little boy is cowering beneath the ox,
and praying whenever there is the slightest sound in the forest,
and many a woman locks the door
if so much as a cuckoo calls on the slope.

The lookouts have dispersed,
and the little gang slips into the hut,
a shelter for the gamekeeper in the days
when these ruins were a castle.
The proud robber feels himself elevated to a knight
upon that rubble where years ago another rogue
once lit his fire.

And when the last footstep echoes away
and the last branch has fallen back with a rustling sound,
it becomes lonely in the forest
where the sun listens out above the branches.
And when the clinking sound inside has come again
and gone on for a little while longer,
silence falls in the hut,
enveloped in the crazed odour of the wine.

The timid bird perches himself
on the roof and shakes his shiny head,
and buzzing through the green of the vines
the wild bee is stealing honey.
Only softly, like a breeze in the pine-tree,
one can hear from inside
the careful whetting
of the knives.

Yes: the maid of the mountains is lovely,
In all the splendour of her firm limbs,
with her undisguised joy
and her raven-black plaits.
If you see her pushing her way through the tangle
of blackberries, so fresh, so sturdy,
you will think the wild rose has leapt
from its stem out of sheer exuberance.

Now she stands still and looks about her -
everywhere only trees and more trees.
Yes, the maid of the mountain is wandering aimlessly in the forest
and hardly realizes it.
Another two minutes, during which she was thinking
and letting her fevered limbs pulsate,
and then, swift as a marten,
she boldly slips down into the quarry.

At the entrance stands a block of rock
overhung by the debris.
Ivy shakes its tresses
and pushes forward its green leaves.
There, beneath that roof, she settles down,
leaning comfortably against the stone,
and thinks to herself: "In truth, I am sitting here
like the little image of a saint in a shrine!"

She is so warm that she loosens her two plaits
with her chubby hand,
and her black hair tumbles down

like the garment of a raven's wings.
"Ah", she thinks, "I am alone!"
The clasp on her bodice bursts open,
but, as motionless as the stone itself,
wild Rieder is standing behind the rock.

He does not see her, only her foot
rocking playfully to and fro like a boat,
and from time to time, the wind's salutation
pushes a lock of hair around the reef.
Yet he thinks he feels the warm movement of her breath,
the touch of the samum,
and senses lost sounds playing round his ears,
like birds of prey in flight,

The air so soft and warm, bathing her
with the intoxicating fragrance of thyme,
she leans back, stretches, and holds out
her arm, her plump arm, from the crevasse.
Then she closes her radiant eyes -
not to sleep, just to rest for an hour.
And so she dozes off, and the danger grows
from one second to the next.

Now everything is quiet - she *was* awake!
But something stirs behind the rock
and Rieder gently, gently,
lifts his pistol from his shoulder,
takes aim against the rock,
and then loosens the blades of his knives,

lifts his foot - what's holding him back?
A cry seems to penetrate the air!

Ha! the signal! He clenches his fist,
and again the shrill cry of the vulture buzzes
in his ears.
Yet still he hesitates, grinding against the reef,
a third time, and he has
seized his weapon - to the cliff! -
so that gravel and sand come rolling down
from the stony skeleton.

And the girl jumps up, too.
"Ah! is the rock so loose?" she asks herself,
and slowly, yawning, she steps out of the
make-believe shrine,
lifting the moist radiance of her eyes
to see the position of the sun.
That is when she sees a vulture flying over
with a lamb between its claws.

Pulling herself together quickly,
child of the wild that she is,
she follows the direction of its flight.
It has come from where there are people,
and that is enough for the maid of the mountains.
But quiet! Is that not the sound of voices
and the clatter of wheels? Be quiet! - she listens!
and, sure enough, the heavy carriage is groaning and creaking
through the pine needles.

"Hi, girl!" comes the cry from the carriage,
and she approaches with a dainty curtsey.
"Show us the way to the village.
 We have got ourselves lost among the pines."
"Sir", she says with a laugh, "take me with you.
I am lost too, but I can guide you."
"Right, you lovely child: climb up!
Just climb in quickly! Are you still hesitating?"

"Sir, I do not know much,
but it will take you to people,
and that is valuable in itself,
in a forest with gangs of robbers in it.
Look, on the top of the mountain
I saw a bird of prey soaring from below,
carrying a lamb in its claws.
There must be a herd there."

In the evening the hero of the forest stands
and curses those stones, both cold and warm.
The money-dealer is happy that he has skilfully guided
his money through the forest.
And only the virtuous, honest maiden does not realize,
as she is overcome by dreams,
that heaven has so mercifully kept its shield
over her that day.

The Death of Archbishop Engelbert of Cologne

The source for this powerful poem, usually regarded as one of the most successful of Droste-Hülshoff's ballads, is a significant event in thirteenth century German history, the death of the politically highly influential Archbishop of Cologne at the hand of a distant relative, Count Friedrich of Isenburg. Their conflict belongs to the power struggles of the Stauffen period, but there was also personal antagonism between them, which arose from Friedrich's sense of having been demeaned and slighted by the ambitious prelate. Into this already complex mix of motivations, Droste-Hülshoff adds another ingredient which must have struck a chord with her readers, for, as he rides towards his death, Engelbert is deep in thoughts of his plans for an extension to Cologne Cathedral. This massive project, begun by him in the 13th Century, and conceived as testimony to his pride in his position and power, was put on hold after his assassination and fulfilled in accordance with his plans some twenty years after his death. When this poem was written, in 1841, and after several further attempts to add to it and enhance its grandeur, the Cathedral was once more the focus of contention and debate which are reflected in her two poems about its chequered history and its role in expressing the eminence of Germany.

All these elements come together in the present poem, but most poignant of all is the final strophe, which expresses the personal tragedy of the man who has been executed for a brutal murder which - and opinions differ on this - he may not really have intended to perpetrate. After the violence of the attack and the struggle and the death throes of the mighty cleric, the final focus, and surely what makes this poem so memorable, is the picture of the widow shooing the ravens away from his place of execution, and her anguished cry; whatever the wider implications of the act, this was a man, her husband, and the father of her young sons.

There is much which is memorable in this fine poem, to which the term 'ballad', though it is used to describe it, does not really apply. If one employs it, then it is with the awareness that Droste-Hülshoff took the concept of the ballad to new heights and made it, through some magnificent examples, very much her own.

The Death of Archbishop Engelbert of Cologne

1
The meadow steams. The Ruhr is seething.
The reeds whistle in the sharp east wind.
Then there is the gentle sound of trotting through the open field,
and something rises up like streaks of mist,
and there is rushing down into the river,
and the shoulders of the horses brace themselves against the waves
as they fly past, their hooves clinging to the ground.

Then a snorting, a leap, and the steed
hurls its wet flanks, and then another,
and two more, until twenty-five are forming a barrier there.
On! On! Over heath and through forest,
until at the point where the thicket forms itself
into a desolate ball they break through the tangled bushes
with a crackling sound.

Isenburg is standing there,
against the trunk of an oak-tree,
out of the wind,
his arm flung round one branch.
He's thinking and dwelling on his memories.
Can he hear what Rinkerad, the pale knight,
is softly whispering, like birdsong through the branches?

"Count" comes the whisper. "Count, hold fast!
It seems to me that it could drive you mad.
By the Blood of Christ,
do not let us return home like whipped dogs!
Who was it who tied your hands,
robbed you of the right to ride free?"
But Isenburg seems not to hear.

"Count" the whisper goes on.
"Who was the man who matched the Rose with the Cross[1)]
and then made your brother-in-law
a stranger in his own land?
And, Count, who mocked at your rights and
labelled you a servant of the priests?"
Isenburg leans against the bough.

"And who, who was it who decreed
that you should stand in the hair shirt of a penitent
with the candle of infamy in your hand
and beg old crones to say
the Kyrie and the Litany for you?"
At that the branch broke in two
and whirled about in the stormy blasts.

Isenburg spoke and said: "My good fellow,
do you think I am dead and buried then?
Oh, just let me get hold of -
But still, be silent! I hear the sound of horses' hooves."
They stand there leaning forward, listening,
and through the trees appear the plumes
and flutter over them like ravens.

2
How frightening is the forest in the gloom
of misty November days!
How strangely does the wilderness echo
with the groaning of the branches
and the sighing of the wind!
"Listen, boy. Was that the sound of weapons?"
"No, gracious lord, only the sound of a
bird, carried on the wings of the storm."

The mighty prelate rides on,
the bold Archbishop of Cologne,
he whom it pleased the Emperor to appoint
as his counsellor and imperial regent,
the iron hand of the clergy,
and two noble youths, two riders, and in addition
three abbots as companions.

Calmly he rides on,
dreaming of the beauty of a splendid cathedral.
With the bridle resting on his horse's neck,
he gently strokes its thick mane.

The wind rises and falls.
There is a shudder when a drop
falls from branch and leaves, a foggy tear.

Already the nave is mounting up to dizzy heights.
Already the twirly edges are forming - then listen!
A whistle, and whoosh! A grip, a plume here,
an arm at his neck!
There's a crashing like a pack of wild boars.
The abbots flee like chaff blown away,
and then riders are attacking riders.

Ha! a despicable battle! two up against ten!
However, the prince has struggled free.
He whips his horse and with a groan
it has hurled itself over the hollow way.
The switch lets out a whistling sound. "Alas, Rinkerad!"
The prelate slides from his horse
and forces his way through the thicket.

"Faster, faster! Kill the dog, the proud dog!"
And a mob races into the forest, forming a circle,
then forwards and backwards, and to the side.
The branches crack - ah!
it's getting close!
Today it is the prelate standing against the tree-trunk,
like a trapped boar.

He casts a desperate look at his sword
and releases the short, broad blade,

then his left hand feels beneath his cloak
to check his chain-mail,
and now - right! - he's ready!
To be sure, the priest fought like a man that day,
and his aim was like a flame.

There's a twanging sound and a ringing through the forest.
The leaves fall like dust from the oak-trees
and soon blood-red trickles are sliding down,
running over his arm and his head.
Yet still the prelate struggles, disarmed though he is,
that powerful man, when a perfidious dagger
thrusts its way with a hissing sound into his side.

Isenburg cries out: "That's enough! It is too much!"
and seizes his reins.
But he saw a servant strike him again and
snatched the wretch by the hair out of his stirrups.
"It is too much! Be gone! Quickly!"
And they are off, and a whirlwind
beats at them from behind, like the wings of an owl.

The storm has subsided,
the drops are glinting on the leaves,
and above the pool of blood the crest of the woodpecker
hearkens from its vantage point.
What is that rustling down from the hill,
dragging itself like a wounded deer?
Ah, poor boy, sick dove!

"My gracious lord, my beloved master,
so the murderers had to attack you like this?
My virtuous one, my saintly one!"
He pulls his little scarf from round his neck
and presses it to the wound, again and again,
here and there.
Ah, wound upon wound, and bloody gashes!

"Ah, ah!" Then he bends down and looks to see
if there is still a breath of life.
Did it not seem as if a sigh crept out?
as if a finger moved?
But there's another sound -Ho! Holla, hola!—Hallo! hoho! -
and he is glad to hear it:
"Our riders are coming from all sides!"

3
At Cologne on the Rhine
a woman is kneeling on the ravens' stone,
beneath the wheel.
And lying across the wheel is a body,
on which graze crows and maggots.
His shield is shattered and his castle in ruins.
His soul is in the mercy of God.

Smoke enfolds the body of the priest,
from lamps and smouldering incense.
Around his body swirls the scent of decay,
and hail beats against the hollows in his ribs.
In the Cathedral a funeral hymn is sung,

and a *Te Deum* for his agony arises
from a thousand voices.

And whenever a citizen sees the wheel
he makes his little horse trot quickly by,
but a pale lady kneels and shoos away the ravens with her kerchief.
For her sake he did not shun the noose.
He was her hero.
He was the light of her life -
and ah! the father of her boys!

[1]Among the grudges that Isenburg bears towards the Archbishop is his refusal to grant his ancestral rights to his brother-in-law, symbolised in his withholding of his family's emblem and appropriating it to himself.

One is left at the end of this poem with a heart-rending sadness, and Droste-Hülshoff seems to achieve this through her own sorrow that two men, each great in his own way, come to an untimely end. She describes the terrible attack in the forest, and the battle that ensues, vividly and without comment on the rights and wrongs of it, beyond the brief comment that it is 'despicable' that two men should be so outnumbered, and the lament "Alas, Rinkerad!"

Perhaps Friedrich von Isenburg would not have had it this way, although he has heard the whispering of his companion, reminding him of the grudges he bears against the Archbishop: who struck the fatal blow was later disputed, though Isenburg paid the terrible price.

Very often in her narrative poems, Droste-Hülshoff refrains from attributing blame. Though often deeply moral, they leave the ultimate judgement open and end on a note of acceptance and regret.

This fateful confrontation between two men so different in their status and aspirations is set against a background which she evokes, as in her lyric poems, with great power: the sights and sounds of the heathland and the forests of the Rhineland, the wind and the mists she knew so well. There is extraordinary economy in her description of the setting, for what matters are the two men who are brought together that day. The third strophe focuses on the Count, leaning against the oak-tree and contemplating 'his memories': but these memories are expanded on by Rinkerad, who points to the ways in which the Count has suffered through the actions of the Archbishop. It is a question of honour: "do not let us return home like whipped dogs", urges Rinkerad, but for the widow, mourning at the place of execution, it is a question of his love for her and her children.

In an echo of that picture of Isenburg deep in his thoughts is the later one of the Archbishop in the thick of the attack, standing against the tree-trunk 'like a trapped boar'. The sword is alien to this man of the Church and the politics of the State, yet he must use it, albeit in vain, and when he draws it he fights 'like a man that day', his aim 'like a flame'. The closest Droste-Hülshoff comes to condemning the murder is when she speaks of the 'perfidious dagger' which delivers the final blow, and it is Isenburg himself who tries to put a stop to the action, although it is too late. It is left to the grieving page to praise his dead master, in a scene which sums up the tragedy in human terms, as he tries in vain to stench the blood.

All that remains now is for this magnificent poem to conclude with two contrasting pictures: of the body of the great cleric lying in the cathedral which had filled his thoughts on that fateful day, receiving the traditional hymns of mourning, the *Te Deum* sung by thousands, and of the wretched corpse of the man judged to have brought about his death, lauded with the simple cries of love from his wife as he lies on the wheel which proclaims his guilt to passers-by who prefer not to pay much heed to him. Temporal values pale beside the eternal, and the souls of both men are in the mercy of God.

The Return of the Mother

'The Return of the Mother' belongs to the same year (1840) as 'The Grey Man', and it too has at its heart a supernatural experience. She mentions them - 'two ballads' - somewhat dismissively in a letter to her dear friend Christoph Schlüter, in which she tells him that she has struck an unproductive period in her creative life, having the ideas but not the ability to express them to her satisfaction (letter dated 28.4.1840). She had, after all, just completed, at least for the time being, the second section of 'The Spiritual Year', and 'The Jew's Beech', and the impact of her burgeoning relationship with Levin Schücking had yet to take effect. This letter to someone very close to her and one in whom she confided throughout her adult life, suggests that she was feeling alone and doubtless tired and somewhat frail in the remote Rüschhaus.

However, these two poems, and a number of the other ballads she produced at about the same time, do not hint at any diminution of vitality as a poet and can readily take their place with the others which critics tend to label 'the Rüschhaus ballads'. 'The 'Return of the Mother', one of her longest ballads, is very powerful, but in a different way again from some of the others of the early 1840s. Its details and innuendos, what she says and what she does not say, make it extraordinarily memorable, benefiting from frequent re-reading which rarely supplies answers to the questions it poses. Of course, it lacks the robust, near comedy, of 'The Grey Man': it speaks in lingering tones of sadness and regret. There is a bleakness about this poem which anticipates the qualities which dominate Droste-Hülshoff's last great ballad 'The Familiar Spirit of the Horse-Dealer', but it lacks that poem's ultimate message of redemption.

'The Return of the Mother' is spoken by the unnamed husband to his wife Marie, and the story it tells extends from his wretched childhood to the present which is blessed by her and her love, yet in which he can still not shake off the memories that haunt him. The final strophe is a kind of bleak epilogue, for he has once revisited his childhood home, it seems by chance when on his travels. The prayers he uttered there were something of a valediction, for he could not bring himself to enter, or to accept the sustenance - a simple glass of water - it might have offered him.

This ending leaves so many questions unanswered and the wise and gentle Marie knows better than to ask any, or ever to refer to this lengthy account, although she is the source of all his happiness and in her he should, one feels, fulfil a future to outbalance the past.

Droste-Hülshoff leaves the reader of this poem with a deep sense of loss and sorrow. This we recognize from some of her most profound lyric poems which seem to plumb the depths of human emotion, but it is possibly only in 'The Sisters' that anything comparable is found in her narrative poems.

It is the smallest details which supply this lasting impression of 'The Return of the Mother', and the restrained passion with which the husband tells his story, having first insisted that his wife keep her distance and not look at him while he does so. The deeply emotional Droste-Hülshoff understands the workings of the human heart and understands its limitations. The man who has so much emotion pent up in him can speak of it now only if he succeeds in doing so with objectivity and sometimes with an acute regard for the facts.

Thus the second strophe lays the facts before us in the simplest terms. His childhood was desperately unhappy because his parents were unhappy in their marriage. However much they may have tried to keep their anger and discord from their children, they failed because their anger and discord dominated the household. The father was clearly often absent, but his return always meant grief for the family.

The father is defined by his profession: he is a merchant, evidently unsuccessful, and deeply embittered in consequence. The mother is defined by her weariness and her coughing, the fragile state that takes her to an early grave, a patient, devout woman whose life is constant suffering. Not for a moment does the adult man attribute blame to her.

The stifling effect of their father's presence is expressed in the freedom they feel when he is not there, and then we learn that there is another member of this strange household, an elderly man who emerges as their only real companion, half-tutor and half-chaplain, and charged with caring for them when their father is away.

Swiftly the death of the mother comes, and Droste-Hülshoff describes very perceptively the effect of this loss on the two boys, although as yet we do not know the identity of the other sibling, a shadowy figure whose main function in the whole sad story is to leave the speaker to his lonely life after the death of the mother and the abrupt departure of the father. When and how this third loss came to him is never told, and all we discover is that the brother also left the home, presumably because he died, although we are not told this, very young. For a time the brothers were inevitably thrown together in their virtually orphaned state, and we can only imagine how close the bond between them must have been. With remarkable insight, Droste-Hülshoff describes how initially they veered between uncontrolled grief and tears, and the exuberant activity of two small boys letting off steam in a house of death.

Thus we reach the description of the first appearance of their dead mother, echoed on the next day by her second visit. It is only when he is describing these two events that the husband addresses his wife specifically again: he notices that she is sceptical, as well she might be, given the twilight hour, and the susceptibility of the recently bereaved. However, the details of those two nights are imprinted on his memory, as is the intervening day, when his father is obsessed with what he believes to be the loss of money and turns the house upside down. Events speed up now, culminating in the wife's summoning her husband to the little closet, although we never know what comes to pass there. Whatever happens leads to his parting from his sleeping sons, and his departure from his home.

The letter he wrote to the chaplain is engraved in the memory of the surviving elder son, but it tells nothing of the circumstances which drive the man from his home and his motherless children. Something has happened which is so terrible that it has driven him to such despair, but we are not to know of it, nor of the fate that befell him. This is the nature of this brilliant poem: much is implied, but most is left unsaid.

The Return of the Mother

"You are always asking me, Marie,
why I flee from my homeland,
although the beloved old images
are still engraved in my heart
A woman should conceal nothing from her husband,
and a man nothing from his faithful wife,
so sit down, I want to tell you something,
but sit apart from me, and do not look at me.

I lived with my parents - a child,
a child and not happy about that.
A harsh wind blew in the house.
Marital harmony fled from there.
I was not allowed to hear quarrels
or angry words, yet they hung over everything like a cliff.
It was a sorry day for us children
when we saw our father returning from his journeys.

A merchant, his stern spirit
embittered by many a loss,
and my mother, she was so weary,
her breast filled with coughing.

I can still see her, her eyes reddened,
a picture of silent, careworn patience,
kneeling and praying at our bedside.
To be sure, my mother was free of guilt.

But when my father was off on his travels,
perhaps in London or Vienna,
we lived again and breathed freely,
and grew as green as cress.
The virtuous chaplain, lean and grey,
who was meant to look after all of us -
for nothing was entrusted to my mother -
made us laugh with his funny tales.

Then heaven sent us a deep sorrow.
She dragged herself around for such a long time
and gently grieved herself into her shroud.
We made parting hard for her.
We were like crazed birds in the glade,
flown from the faithful nest too early,
now racing madly around over blocks and stones,
now cowering in the corner.

The old man, the worthy chaplain,
grew hot and cold,
if he saw us coming soiled with dust and sweat
and glowing like ovens,
but when we entered the deserted room
and saw the little stool at the piano,
uncontrolled grief burst forth
and we cried for our mother.

On the sixth evening after she had gone -
we were huddled over the fire,
the old man was leaning against the mantelpiece
watching the coals smouldering,
we were not speaking, we were too upset -
the door in the hallway groaned softly
and we heard footsteps shuffling towards us.
My little brother cried out: "Mother is here!"

"Quiet! just be quiet!" We all listened,
pressed close to one another and afraid.
We distinctly heard the sound of footsteps
echoing along the creaking floor.
We clearly heard the chairs being moved,
the bunch of keys clinking in the cupboard,
and then the heavy cracking of the floorboards,
as this Something stepped from the chair to the ground.

My young blood was coursing through my veins.
I could see the old man clinging like stone
to the edge of the mantelpiece
as It slowly entered.
Oh, God! I saw my mother, Marie!
Marie, I saw my mother walking in her simple dress,
just as she used to come early in the morning
to see her two little boys.

Her gaze was firmly turned towards the ground:
thus did she sway through the room,
the bunch of keys in her pale hand,

her eyes dull as opal.
She raised her arm and we heard a squeaking sound,
just like a key turning in the lock,
and then we saw her slip into the cupboard
where we kept our money and our silver.

You can probably imagine
that not a breath broke the awful desolation,
and it was certainly silent in the cupboard too.
We listened and listened for a long time.
Then I saw the old man fall,
and his forehead hit the stonework.
At that we let out a cry
and our servants came rushing in.

You say nothing to me, Marie,
yet I do not doubt that you are shaking your head:
an old man, two children, twilight.
Imagination is at work in such circumstances.
What would I not give for your smiles,
for your doubts, you virtuous woman,
but I'll say it again. By my very life, Marie,
this was exactly what we saw and heard.

Next morning father returned home,
In a bad mood and worn out.
And while he was never honey,
now he was wormwood,
and the words he spoke to the old man
were certainly questionable,

for they argued loudly at the gate
and parted very resentfully.

Now the whole house was turned upside down,
everyone questioned, grilled,
the money-bags were weighed and shaken out,
the silver cutlery counted,
checking whether everything was in order, the rooms locked.
Still nothing satisfied the man and
he was counting and weighing again and again until evening,
believing, he said, that the loss would still be uncovered.

When twilight approached,
without our mother and without the chaplain,
we cowered on the dusty stone
and stared yawning into the flames.
In a bad mood, our father rummaged in papers
at the long table, pushing and pulling.
We crouched against our fireplace like fishes
when the eye of the heron bears down upon them.

Then listen! The door creaked in the passage, and
shuffling footsteps dragged their way
over the cracking floorboards.
Father listened - stood up - and again
we heard the chairs being moved,
the bunch of keys jingling at the cupboard,
and again the heavy crunching of the floorboards,
as It stepped from the chair down to the ground.
He stood, his body bent over,
like a huntsman on the track of his prey.

There was no fear, no emotion, in his eyes,
and one could see that he was just waiting.
And again I saw the woman who had given birth to me
banished, pushed out of the holy ground.
Oh, I have never forgotten that night:
it will follow me to the hour of my death.

And he? Moved not an eyelid,
twitched not a muscle,
and only once gently moved the chair
on which he had been resting his hand.
Following her with his piercing gaze
he turned slowly as she walked away,
but when he saw her pressing on the cupboard
he started up, as if he wanted to go with her.

And "Arnold!" came the cry from the money dungeon,
and he bent over, far over,
and again "Arnold!", so pitifully sweet.
He laid down his pen.
Then a third time, like the bloody cry of mourning,
"Arnold!" He seized his meerschaum in a flash,
hurled it against the wall,
then went into the closet, and bolted it.

But we rushed out into the sunset
in a frenzy,
We had seized one another's hands
and wept ourselves almost to death.
The lamp burned the whole night.

The embers in the fireplace in the room
crackled and when the third evening came
Father settled himself at his post.

I did not say my farewells to him,
did not kiss his hand,
but it is said that that night
he stood by our little cot.
And at first light the next morning
the first thing I saw
was the chaplain, shocked to the core,
kneeling at our bedside.

A letter had been brought to him
in the early morning,
and then a little key, too.
"I will not read it", he thought,
and he hesitated, but then after all he did read the letter,
written in his final hour in my unhappy father's hand,
a letter which has remained firmly in my heart,
although my brother burnt it at some point.

"I will not say what has befallen me -
my tongue will wither away before I do so,
but it is a bitter, heavy judgement,
and it drives me from my house and home.
In the closet are papers, bills of exchange,
along with letters,
and I commend to you my two boys,
for you are a loyal man.

Do not worry about me.
I have enough of what I need,
and do not ever try to find me.
I am warning you in all earnestness:
it would not bring you the truth.
Be calm, my friend. I will not kill the body that has still much to endure,
but see to it that my poor little children pray,
for I have urgent need of the prayers of the innocent."

And in the closet a proper will was found,
and all the papers ordered and carefully labelled,
according to the manner of a merchant.
And we? They had us cared for in foreign parts,
and we were just like other boys,
but as the years passed
circumstances changed
and I am now his only child.

You know how hard it was for me
to lose my brother so young, too,
and if I did not have you, my Marie,
I should be a poor fool.
Ah God! What did I not write in my anguish,
appeals, letters!
But all in vain, always in vain.
Is he still alive? - probably dead!"

Never again did the good Marie
bring back to his tragic story
the husband who now found

his only happiness in her.
She offered him her hands, so gentle and so protective,
and gave him several splendid children,
so that in the end the dark creases
vanished from his honest brow.

To be sure, after many years, his way
once brought him close to his home,
and he requested a stop
and gazed at the towers.
With his hands folded, he seemed to be praying,
but then - a wave - and the carriage rattled on.
He did not ever enter that place
and never took a drink of water there.

Kurt von Spiegel

The issue of guilt and expiation of guilt, and of the administering of justice in this world, recurs in Droste-Hülshoff's ballads, even when she does not herself pronounce judgement or suggest that her reader is meant to adopt a particular standpoint. Most frequently what she does is present the facts and leave open the verdict they may invite on human behaviour. In 'Retribution', it is clear what she means, though she modified her original title, which placed the punishment the passenger receives for his action firmly in the hands of God. It is fate which intervenes to ensure that this should be the case, even if the punishment is conducted through human agency.

In 'Kurt von Spiegel' her view seems to be less clear, or, rather, she appears to leave open whether she approves or disapproves of the summary justice administered long after the event by the new bishop. What she allows him to do is express his regret that his office requires him to act as he does, that justice must take its course, and certainly take precedence over the claims of kinship. She does not ponder upon the rights and wrongs of such an office, as the poem ends with the swift execution of Spiegel, although perhaps there is just a hint of a negative attitude in her emphasis on the overtly Christian trappings of the Mass, the breviary and the *inful* of the priest.

The picture she has built up of Kurt von Spiegel is a wholly negative one. His killing of the innocent painter on the roof of the castle is a thoroughly despicable act, born of irritation that he has been unsuccessful in the hunt that day. It is the result of spite and pride, and that pride has already been emphasised in the opening lines, which actually blame the old Bishop for allowing the arrogant Spiegel to assume a position of rank dependent on his inflated opinion of his status and not, as quickly becomes evident, because he had any personal qualities to merit his rise to power.

This poem has its source in Westphalian history and was written during Droste-Hülshoff's stay, mostly on her own, in the Rüschhaus near Münster. In some ways it resembles ballads of an earlier period, in its robust account of a single episode which leads to another single episode, and then to another, and in the almost caricature presentation of its central figures. Above all, the larger-than-life Kurt von Spiegel dominates the action, and determines the events. It lacks the subtlety of other poems of the same time, and cannot be said to be remarkable save inasmuch as it represents another side of her skill in narration. If one places it side by side with poems of the same period in her development, as in this selection, one may find it somewhat unsubtle and relatively disappointing. Most critics who write of her work tend to slide over it, and this is probably not surprising. However, it deserves to be included in this selection of her ballads precisely for the reasons implied: that it demonstrates another aspect of her talent for telling a story, in this case with some vigour, and that it shows what a wide range she had in her choice of subject and in her ways of handling her subjects.

The poem consists of a series of vivid scenes which join up to form this account of the rise and fall of a named individual known to history and doubtless rooted in her knowledge of her locality. There is nothing subtle about it, and it raises no profound issues which tax the thinking and feeling of the reader. The first scene of the hunt is colourful and noisy, and it ends with the angry Spiegel deliberately deciding to vent his anger and disappointment on the wretched painter, who has absolutely nothing to do with his failure to get what he wanted from the day. If we are called upon to think about the injustice of this action, the power of the strong over the weak, and the inequality of an unfair society, then this is not stressed, and it is not what the poem is about. The harmless man falls to the ground clutching his wretched little hat, and although the Bishop, who sees it happen, is horrified, he does nothing to stop Spiegel escaping, although he utters the threat of death which his successor will act upon in years to come. The arrogance of Spiegel is confirmed as he smiles complacently on the vassals who are likewise appalled by what they have seen but powerless to take action. The portcullis closes, but too late to prevent his escape.

The years pass unnumbered and what happens in them is not recounted. Only one thing changes: the old Bishop is replaced by a new one, but this one bears on his *inful*, the headband of his office, an emblem that indicates that he belongs to the same family as Spiegel. Already as he takes up his place in the Cathedral he is aware that upon him rests a task handed on to him by his predecessor, but it is Spiegel himself who provides the opportunity. Arrogant as ever, for the years appear to have taught him nothing, he presumes that the kinship he has with the new incumbent will protect him. Once again he acts with no thought for any consequences when he appears at a public gathering, the focus of all eyes, stained with the blood of his innocent victim.

If there is a hero in this poem, then it is the newly consecrated Bishop who does not for a moment forget the onus that lies upon him. The echo of the past comes with Droste-Hülshoff's repetition of the same command to the bystanders: 'seize him, seize him'. What happens then is irrelevant and left untold. The man has been condemned all those years before and the sentence is carried out without delay. There is no sympathy for Spiegel himself.

Kurt von Spiegel

Oh, pious prelate, how could you allow the foolish vanity
of the Marshall to climb so high!
Was it his figure, whose nobility deceived you,
his fluttering wit among cups and dancing?
Oh, pious bishop, what were you thinking of
when your reluctant silence passed judgement on
innocent blood smouldering on the meadow?

The forest cry of triumph resounds on the Wewelsburg.
Foam from the horse's flanks runs down over his stirrups.
The deer coughs and, close to the noble beast,
a fleeting mastiff,
coughs Kurt von Spiegel.
From the top of the tower the wretched painter listens
and, in his hand, he holds the crumbling tile.

Then listen! 'mort!'. The hunt is over,
the single tear of the deer is shed,[1)]
and a blast on the horns brings all the shaggy company
through the forest to the entrails.
And soon out of the nodding branches
come the silent beaters, the mass of riders,
and slowly make their way onwards with their groaning horses.

Spiegel spurs on his foaming beast:
"Damn scoundrels, you have robbed me!" Then,
high up on the crenellated tower,
he sees the wretched painter on the swaying planks
"Ah", he grumbles, "No spoils, not a shot, today.
I have never before returned home so humiliated.
I'll get that sparrow over there all right."

The painter sees him blinking upwards
and makes a grab for his wretched little hat,
then he sees the shotgun being aimed down below
and then he hears the crack, and then the bullet whistling.
"Got him, got him!" He reels and turns about,
then tumbles down along with the tile, and the plank,
and all his tools, on to the grassy patch.

The prelate jerks, as though he had received the deadly shot,
and his eyes are glinting.
"Marshall!" he groans, and his forehead is wet, and
on his swelling throat the lumps are quivering.
Then a red glow comes over his cheek, and he cries "Marshall,
this will be your death. Get him, get him,
you beaters and guards of mine."

But the Spiegel smiles down from his steed,
and smiles round at the ashen vassals.
"My noble lord", he says, "not too loud, not too loud!
Your threats will echo in the wind."
Then swiftly he turns and races at great speed
through the gate and up the thundering bridge.
Too late the grilles have descended, too late!

In the Cathedral at Paderborn the funeral bells
have tolled out for the old prelate, and once again
in the Cathedral the authority of the Chapter has
elected and decreed the new ruler.
The new bishop journeys in silence through mountains and fields
to the Wewelsburg,
accompanied by the murmuring of his retinue.

And when he comes rolling across the bridge
and sees the vast towers stretching upwards,
how his heart trembles and groans!
On his bishop's headband- oh, fiery spot! -
the blood of Spiegel bright on the family tree,
he lets out a soft sigh and quickly murmurs:
"My lord Steward, let us now lay our table."

131

The goblets are circulated, and the cannons crack -
stately knights and charming ladies - the pleasant ball
of light-heartedness is tossed about,
and all this has almost removed the creases from his forehead
when - listen! - footsteps come hurrying in the hall,
and doors are creaking, and a tall figure, Spiegel,
the bloodstained Marshall, is standing in the doorway.

The Bishop looks as white as a shroud,
and there is not a breath to be heard in the vast hall.
At once he covers his eyes with his right hand
and then slowly lets it fall to his side.
He sighs, hollowly, grimly, heavily:
"Kurt! Kurt von Spiegel! What are you doing here?
Seize him, you vassals of mine, seize him!"

No sinner's bell was rung,
No scaffold was built and carried there.
Yet there came the harsh sound of seven shots cracking out,
and a Mass was said.
The Bishop gazed at the blood-stained stone,
then softly murmured into his breviary:
"Heavy it is indeed, to wear a bishop's headband."

[1])The deer was said to weep only in its dying moments.

Second Sight

In that winter at the Rüschhaus in 1840-41, Droste-Hülshoff
was extraordinarily busy and, spending so much time alone, or

in the company of her faithful Maria Kathrin, and on her long walks in the neighbourhood, she must have been much occupied with thoughts of her homeland and her origins in it, and of the nature of the surrounding countryside and its people. These thoughts were undoubtedly feeding into the work she was producing at the request of Levin Schücking for his own work, together with his friend Ferdinand Freiligrath, which was beginning to appear as illustrated 'Images of Westphalia' and to which Droste-Hülshoff made substantial contributions. Although these began as accounts in prose on the nature of the countryside and its impact on the thinking and lore of the people there, it was already evident to the surprisingly percipient Schücking that, as he was to put it very soon, her true genius lay in lyric poetry. Thus, increasingly, she was contributing much more and in a different way from the original concept, and although the nature of this serialised publication probably demanded that her name be concealed, it was in this way that some of her ballads first became known to a wider audience. Once she had assembled a large corpus of work, and, with the aid of Schücking, the poems had formed an important part of the 1844 edition, her career, albeit late in the day, was established.

This provenance is significant, for it accounts for the fact that so many of the narrative poems of these years are based in the history of Westphalia, and that they frequently reflect her own leaning towards superstition and the supernatural.

When she opens 'Second Sight' with a series of questions, she is pointing towards matters very close to her heart. She knows these people with their striking fair hair and piercing blue eyes, precisely the physical features noted by anyone who described her; they are her neighbours and she is one of them. She feels herself, and always has done, a member of that 'tormented race'. It is in part this understanding that distinguishes 'Second Sight' from, for example, the much more traditional 'Kurt von Spiegel', written at about the same time.

This is the Droste-Hülshoff who can reflect, in 'The Fräulein of Rodenschild', on a spine-chilling experience almost certainly her own, or, in 'The Return of the Mother' understand how the child grew up to be a man, a husband and a father, but could recall in minute detail the events of those two evenings which changed his life forever and from which he could never recover.

Artistically, what is so striking is her ability to change the mood and the tempo of her poems, and to find her inspiration in such a varied range of material. Waller in 'The Grey Man' may leave that night behind and go about his everyday business, but his hair is ice-grey now, and the reader must recall that the near-burlesque of a rowdy evening of over-indulgence and the mocking of the ancestral portraits on his bedroom wall were juxtaposed with a terrifying and unexplained tussle in the middle of the night and a shot which passed mysteriously unheard. The Fräulein of Rodenschild always keeps a glove on her hand, yet she dances away at balls in the castle and appears to have recovered from the illness that once befell her. The somewhat limited and literally-minded Adèle Schopenhauer who questioned this apparently unlikely behaviour after such a powerful experience would also have liked to know what it was that the girl in 'The Cry of the Vulture' had managed to escape. Clearly, for all her aspirations to literary judgement and her undoubted devotion to her friend, she sometimes failed to recognize - and one can but assume that there were other occasions that remain unrecorded - that Droste-Hülshoff's is a rare genius, one which encompasses so much and probes so deeply, and even sometimes says much by saying nothing.

When she begins 'Second Sight' with this explicit link to her homeland, she is making an unmistakable reference to the reputation of its people for powerful psychic sense. The core of this poem, like that of 'The Fräulein of Rodenschild', is a real event, based in this case not on a personal experience but on an account she had read in the course of her research. In 'Das malerische und romantische Westfalen' ('Picturesque and romantic Westphalia', compiled by Ferdinand Freiligrath and Levin Schücking) in which this poem made its first appearance, she supplies the information that it is based on a premonition recounted by Baron Caspar von Kerkering zur Borg (1713-1746) and supplies the further information essential to an understanding of the impact of what is described here, that the coffin of a child would bear the emblems of both his parents. At the high point of drama of the poem, her readers, who may or may not have already known this significant detail, are provided with the explanation of the near-panic of the Baron as he demands that the bearers turn the coffin, but then of his cry of thanks to God, and his calm action in preparing to write his will in the middle of that turbulent night.

It is altogether a poem of intense drama, but drama expressed with great deliberation and control. This is Droste-Hülshoff at the height of her powers, one feels, addressing a theme very close to her own heart and mind. In her greatest ballads - and this must surely rank as one of them - she exploits the drama that Goethe saw as one of the essentials of the ballad, but not necessarily the drama that expresses itself in action, although she is capable of that, as we have seen, for example, in her account of the ambush and ensuing murder of the Archbishop of Cologne, or that moment when Kurt von Spiegel confronts the court in all his confidence and arrogance. She is just as brilliant when she is probing the workings of the human mind and human emotions.

Much of the impact of this poem depends on the atmosphere that pervades this experience from the very beginning: the moonlight touches the hair of the Baron as he sleeps, and bears down upon him like the tongue of a vampire. He can no more escape it than he can subsequently avoid the patches of light on the floor as he paces desperately up and down the corridors of his castle. This is the poison that he feels, and it is the poison of fear. It is described as being like a creature ready to clutch him in its claws and take him towards the window, from which he will witness the funeral procession. In another powerful image, she describes him as being like a stag, proud and splendid, but hunted, until he can be hunted no more and ends up clinging desperately to his own bedpost in his own bedchamber.

Now, at this central point of the poem, the reason for his anguish is disclosed. His only child is ailing, and his wife is dead; the future of the dynasty is at stake. The description of the family tree which he placed at the foot of the boy's bed when he lovingly took leave of him the night before holds the key to the dénouement of the poem, when he will see that only roses adorn the emblems on the coffin. He himself is soon to die, but at least the family line will be assured.

Meanwhile he has yet to see the procession in the courtyard below, clearly the members of his own household, and he no longer avoids the window and the moonlight in his urgent need to learn the message of his vision. The master of the house is a good man, it seems clear, and his servants all have a place in his household. The tiny detail of the plaster on the hand of the steward tells of the imminence of the events which are to unfold. His main concern, however, is with one piece of evidence: he needs to know whose horse has been 'nailed according to ancient custom'. However much he stares he seems not to receive an answer, for now the coffin itself takes all his attention, as he concentrates on the emblems upon it. Again the moonlight plays its part, making the escutcheons glint as the bearers slowly turn it. The vision has given him his answer, and it is another light, the lamp of his own home, by which he writes his will. Shorter than many of her ballads, this example of her mature work is so effective because it is compressed, but still it manages to express so much tension which subsides only when the truth is revealed and the Baron accepts this truth calmly in the knowledge that the dreadful alternative, the death of his only child, has been averted.

Second Sight

Do you know the pale people in the heathland
with their blond, flaxen hair?
with eyes so clear,
like the waves flashing at the edge of the pond?
Oh, say a prayer, devout and true,
for the watchers of the night, the tormented race.

The air so clear that not even the slightest wisp
dreams in the pure firmament.

The full moon casts a blue light
on the hair of the sleeping baron,
the vampire's tongue, the shaft of the ray,
boring downwards with its cold strength.

The sleeper groans. An anguished dream
seems to torment his senses.
His eyelids tremble, and a slight redness
begins to creep across his cheek.
See how he heaves and rows and moves,
like someone battling against the current.

Now he starts up - has he been dreaming?
He cannot remember.
He's freezing, freezing cold, although inside him
there's a surging, like waters hurtling towards a whirlpool.
And he knows what it was that struck fear into him:
it was the poisonous breath of the moon.

Oh, curse of the heathland! To wander
like Ahasver[1] beneath the starry night-sky,
when the darting sea of its rays bores into
the sluice-gates of the soul,
and the prophet, a desperate savage,
struggles against the slowly mounting image.

Shivering in his cloak the baron paces
the length and breadth of the wooden floor,
and wherever there is a patch of light shining on the ground
he walks well to the side of it.

He has his own desire and his own power,
and these shall not end in the fangs of blood.

It is trying to seize him in its claws;
it is sucking him to where the light
is glancing across the window panes,
but moving step by step as a wounded stag proceeds,
hunted into an ever-decreasing circle,
he at last grips the bed-post.

He stands there gasping for breath, thinking, thinking,
trying to calm his weary soul.
He thinks of his beloved only child,
his frail, sickly boy,
above whose life the father's prayer
hangs like a trembling flame.

Did he not place the child's ancestral tree
at the foot of the bed,
and fervently fold his hands over it
after the night-time kiss and blessing?
Flickering in the moonlight the parchment displays
shield upon shield, with absolutely no end to them.

Down the right-hand side his own dynasty,
the ancient baronial emblems,
three roses pale against a silver background,
two pages, wolves bearing shields,
and rose upon rose opening and blossoming,
just like the canopy that glows above the prince.

And on the left the dynasty of the gentle mother,
the pious lady in her tomb,
with arrows darting across blue skies, as though in combat.
The baron sighs, his forehead bowed,
and before he has time to think,
he is standing at the window.

Caught, caught in the cold rays!
Caught up in the veil of mist,
pressed tight against the oval of the window,
with droplets running down the glass,
his clear eyes, like those of a water-sprite,
fallen prey to the torment of the heath in the breath of the moon.

What a seething mass - he must see it!
What a muttering sound- he must hear it!
But he must stand there like a pillar,
unable to move or turn.
In the courtyard a dark mass is buzzing
and individual sounds rise up.

Hey! A torch! It's dancing about,
bowing and climbing upwards in arching movements,
and an army of flames has filled the vast hall,
nodding and sending forth sparks.
Figures all in black, in mourning attire,
brandish their torches aloft.

And all of them lined up against the wall,
the baron knows them all.

This one has adjusted his shotgun so often,
that one tended the horses in the stable,
and for the one who is emptying his bottle so merrily
he has provided for seventeen years.

And now the worthy steward,
with the broad mourning ribbon on his hat:
he sees him approaching slowly,
shuffling along like a broken rod.
He still has a plaster on his parched old hand,
burnt only yesterday in the heat of the stove.

Ah! and now the horse! coming out through the stable door,
in black drapings and funeral crepe.
Is it Achilles, his own faithful beast,
or is it his son's Medore?
He stares and stares, and now he can also see
that it is limping, nailed according to ancient custom. [2)]

Along the castle-wall the orchestra,
the trumpets muffled in crepe,
is trying out soft cadences,
like the whispering of dreaming breezes.
Then all is quiet. Oh horror! Oh torment!
The coffin is coming out through the gate of the castle.

How vividly do the crests show off their colours
against the black velvet of the drape!
Ah! rose upon rose, the fount of death
has sprayed bloody sparks.

The baron clings to the grille
and then he groans: "-The other side!"

At that the bearers turn slowly,
and the escutcheons glint in the moonlight.
"Oh," sighs the baron, "Thanks be to God!"
No arrow, no arrow! Only roses!
Then slowly he lights the lamp
and in that night he writes his will.

[1]Ahasver, the Wandering Jew of legend and literature, cursed to walk the earth until the Second Coming.

[2]Droste-Hülshoff would have been familiar with the custom of rendering the steed of the deceased lame in order that its limping should contribute to the poignancy of the funeral procession.

The Founder

By the time Droste-Hülshoff wrote this poem, in the summer of 1842, she was in Meersburg, but the source of it lies far back in her youth in Westphalia when she had spent some weeks in the winter of 1819-20 in Wehrden on the Weser, not far from Paderborn, with some distant relatives, the Wolff-Metternichs. Her health was not good at the time, as was increasingly the case now, but, as was her habit, she was able to store up information for future reference and for her use when she was working on the *Images of Westphalia*. The founder of the House was Hermann Werner von Wolff-Metternich zur Gracht, Fürstbischof of Paderborn from 1683 until his death in 1704.

In an instalment of the *Picturesque and Romantic Westphalia* in 1842 she relates a story which was circulating in the village of Wehrden when she was there and to which, with the encouragement of Levin Schücking, she then gave more permanent significance in this ballad, which belongs very much to the years which spanned the virtual end of her time in the Rüschhaus and her first long stay in Meersburg. These years, from 1840 until not long before her death in 1848, include her highly-significant relationship with Schücking and the composition of some of her most important lyric poems. She was truly finding her way as a poet of stature, and 'The Founder', for all its many similarities to 'Second Sight', has a powerful lyric quality not always evident with this intensity and so consistently in her narrative poems.

At the heart of this poem is the story Annette had heard all those years before, of how the old Bishop had sat night after night at his desk in the tower of the Castle where the light from his lamp had cast a bluish light over everything, so that the tower looked like a huge lighthouse. Upon that small detail, current as she says among the children of the village over a century later, she builds this impressive poem. She imagines that the old man might have sat there contemplating what he had achieved, a Castle and the foundation of a dynasty, and these are the thoughts that fill the mind of another old man, Sigismund, the servant left alone to guard the young squire while the family is away and conscious of his responsibility for protecting this young heir.

The setting is powerfully evoked, even more so than in 'Second Sight', which this slightly later poem resembles closely. However, whereas in 'Second Sight' the focus is on the premonition of the Count who sees the ghostly procession in the courtyard beneath his window and knows that it speaks of his death, the hazy apparition which seems to hover in the room, coughing and tapping its way along the corridor, could just as easily be a figment of the imagination of old Sigismund, as he sits there alone with his thoughts and reacts to all the noises of the night around him. It is, after all, the night of the new moon, a night dark and mysterious and conducive to thoughts of the spectre of the ghostly white lady.

The ever-observant Droste-Hülshoff conveys the sights and sounds of the night as brilliantly here as she does in the many other poems of her mature years, though here they form the background to a narrative she tells with great skill, linking her description of the setting with the emotions of the old servant, steeped in the history of the House he serves and deeply aware of his own role within it. He knows, of course, that one hundred years ago to the day the Prince-Bishop was lying on his bier, with the symbols of his eminence beside him, and that the very different sounds of the anniversary requiem Mass have been heard that very day. The bat which hovers outside the window today recalls the time over a century ago when the mighty Bishop sat in the great hall of the Castle and wrote his chronicle, that same great volume which the 'frail old fellow' reads today and hastily returns to the drawer when he thinks he hears the family returning. On edge because of the late hour, the solitude, the memories evoked by the Mass earlier in the day and his consciousness of his weighty task of caring for the child who has fallen asleep and whom he would not wish to rouse abruptly by making a move himself, it is small wonder that his imagination, if that is all it is, is alert and plays tricks on his eyes and ears.

Droste-Hülshoff leaves it open whether he really sees any apparition, or whether the 'something' that glides into the room in a haze and seems to prepare a quill as if to write is conjured up by his heightened sensitivity and the circumstances of the night. It does not really matter how one answers that question. This is the Droste-Hülshoff who was herself acutely aware of the potential for strange happenings and did not, for example, shrink from revealing that, like the Fräulein of Rodenschild, she had seen her double walking down the staircase in the family home in the middle of the night and who, in her poetry, could transform landscapes and even human experiences. The companions who spent the night under the same roof as Waller may have dismissed his thoughts the next morning, but they were not slow to leave the mill which had once been a castle and where the portraits of ancestors line the walls, and Waller's blond hair was icy grey from that time on.

As a person Annette von Droste-Hülshoff was open from her childhood to accepting events which others might have mocked or shunned, and as a poet, she could present them in a way which made clear that anything was possible and that she was the last person to adopt a dogmatic stance.

The present poem is many-layered, and all the more impressive for that. Past and present are seen as parallel; there are two main characters, the Bishop and the old retainer, and they are linked both by the Chronicle, and by the sleeping boy, the heir to the future and the new branch of the dynasty so jealously cherished by the Founder a hundred years before. Sights and sounds have dual significance: the tower that looks like a lantern, and the snorting of the swans, which for a fleeting moment sounds like oars rowing across the moat. Everything is seen from the perspective of the vigilant servant, yet equally from that of the wise Prince-Bishop of earlier days. Yet all this coalesces in the relief and sheer exuberance when the present asserts itself and the lamp in the corridor replaces the distorting light of the moon. The family has returned, and normality has replaced uncertainty.

The Founder

A pale streak of light is floating in the west.
The evening star is shining
above the statue of St George at the gateway.
The nearby moor breathes forth a heavy mist.
Swans, drunk with sleep, softly encircle the island,
where the grey watchtower rises out of the rushes
and the water reeds.

On the roof of the tower the bat moves up and down,
and opens up
the ribbed umbrella of its wings,
and with the whirring sound of an arrow in flight,
it makes its way along the pool, now up, now down again,
then clings against the framework of the window,
and peers into the great hall of the castle,

a vast chamber, adorned in silks and velvets,
where once upon a time the mighty prelate wrote
the chronicle of the house.
The canopy is fresh as ever,
and the green table at which he sat,

146

and over in the chapel today
they sang his requiem Mass.

It is precisely one hundred years today
since he was lying on his bier,
with his cross and his silver staff.
For a hundred years today his eternal lamp
has been burning on his grave.
In his chair against the wall
a frail old fellow sits today.

Sigismund, the servant of the house,
is waiting here for the family, hour after hour.
Night has already come with its veils of mist.
Often he believes he hears the coach,
squeaking on the gravel of the drive.
He sits up - but no - it is only the evening wind
blowing through the pine trees.

It is a dark night, just right
for fantasies and the white lady.
It's become too long for the young squire,
and he is sleeping there behind the damask curtains.
The old man is still holding the chronicle
and turning the pages in the dark, yet
in his ear comes the sound as though of singing:

"Thus I built this castle,
put into it all that I had achieved,
for the benefit of the dynasty which was to care for it.

A new branch will grow forth from the old one.
May God bless it! May God make it great!"
The old man listens attentively and gently pushes the book
from his lap into the drawer.

But no! It was only the bat flying in at the window and out again,
with its shrill sound.
And now it shoots away. The old man leans on the window ledge.
How the pond stretches out around the island,
where the circular watchtower casts it deep shadow
in the dark waters.
The reeds crackle, the toad groans.

There, the old man is thinking.
There the old prelate watched and waited,
When night stretched itself out across the pond.
There he shot the heron
and watched the building of the castle,
his habit white, his grey eyes peering
over the bars of the windows

How shyly the moon is shining!
It must be hiding behind the fir tree.
Does the tower not look like a lantern,
expiring in the distant mist?
How the blue vapour rises in the reeds,
and curls upwards against the window sill!
How strangely the stars are twinkling today!

But, ah! he blinks and strains his eyes,

for the haze is swirling more and more densely,
as if a wick were slowly being fanned into life,
and a grey light were becoming enflamed
in the room in the tower,
and yet, and yet: did he not read in the almanac
that today there was a new moon?

What is that? - clearly, yet made indistinct
by the vapour that forces its way back and forth,
is a table, a light in the middle of the tower,
and now, just like a shadow on the wall,
something steps forward,
raises its arm, moves its hand,
and now it has glided towards the table,

and it sits down, slowly, stiffly.
What is that in its hand? - a streak of white -
and now it pulls something from its sheath
and fiddles with it with both hands -
something like a little stick -
and makes a movement to and fro upon it,
as though sharpening a quill.

The servant blinks and blinks into the distance,
the apparition is swaying and fading away,
but he can still see it dipping the quill,
and something sliding over it like sparks,
and at that very moment everything
has sunk into the element of that dark night
which leaves no trace.

Still Sigismund is standing there,
still staring at the round watch tower.
He thinks he hears the sound of the surface of the pond
stirring as he leans right over the windowsill.
An oar? No, it is the swans moving, and
he has just heard them softly exchanging deep snorts
along the green bank.

He closes the window: "Light! O light!"
But he does not wish to seize the young squire
out of his sleep so suddenly,
still less leave him in the room.
Gently he settles himself in his chair
and pulls out his coral rosary.
"What's that clinking over there against the cups?"

No: it is a fly buzzing in the glass.
The old man's brow is wet.
The furniture resembles tombstones as it stands there.
There is movement and a rattling sound in the room.
Gradually the door opens,
and at that moment
the hound barks at the gateway.

The old man cowers down
and listens with conflicting thoughts.
Yes - a gentle brushing sound on the wooden floor,
like weasels creeping towards the staircase,
and then more and more firmly, tap, tap,
like feet going up and down in sandals.
It's coming! It's getting close! He hears it coughing.

His chair creaks - his brain is in a whirl.
And there's a breath close to his forehead.
At that he starts up and steps back wildly,
seizes the child in blind delight
and hurtles along the corridor.
Ah! Thanks be to God! A light in the passageway!
And the carriage comes rattling across the bridge!

Retribution

This stark ballad belongs to that fruitful period of 1841-42 and presents us with yet another example of Droste-Hülshoff's extraordinary variety of substance and treatment of her material.

Two quite separate sources merge in this poem, actually unconnected with one another and neither addressed in specific detail by Droste-Hülshoff. The one is the sinking of the ship *Batavia* on her maiden voyage in 1629, and the other is the moral issue known as the 'plank of Carneades' after the Greek philosopher (c.155 BC) to whom it is attributed as an example of a judicial dilemma. Both names and both situations would have been known to her readers, but what she does is link them without actual reference to them as her sources and create a powerful poem which is all her own and which continues themes which preoccupy her repeatedly throughout her narrative work: the themes of guilt and punishment, of expiation of sin, and, within that, the roles of chance and the overriding hand of a divine power.

The story it relates can be swiftly told: in a shipwreck a sick man is saved by the fact that he is lying on a plank, a piece of wood from the ship, but he is hurled from this in an encounter with a passenger on the doomed ship and perishes in the waves. The passenger survives long enough to be picked up by a ship and rejoices at his freedom. Three months later, it transpires that the ship which saved his life was in fact a pirate ship, whose murderous crew is condemned to death, and he with them, despite his protestations that he did not belong with them.

Although she does not spell it out, the message is clear: the man receives his just reward for a selfish and wicked act. That is retribution, but her original title spoke of this as justice delivered by the Hand of God ('Die Vergeltung. Gottes Hand'). As surely as in 'The Cry of the Vulture', Providence is at work to ensure a just outcome: the young girl avoids whatever fate seems to have been pending, and the passenger is rewarded with death for his action. In both cases, Droste-Hülshoff changed her original title, and left it to the reader to ponder the source of the outcome. In both cases, however, her own view is clear: that Providence protects the innocent and the 'chance' cry of the vulture that prevents a crime and releases the girl is matched in this slightly later poem with an ironic turn of events, when the condemned man on the gallows sees that these are made of wood from the shipwrecked vessel, or even from the actual plank from which he tossed the sick man. The irony of both narratives is evident, the one couched in the slightly humorous tone of 'The Cry of the Vulture', the other unambiguously stating the grim message that the passenger receives his just deserts. Providence - or is it the hand of God? - is at work in both.

Repeatedly, as one reads the narrative poems of Annette von Droste-Hülshoff, one finds oneself marvelling that the same mind should have been drawn to such a wide range of subject matter, and that the same hand should have produced such diverse textures in the writing.

Nothing softens the tale told in 'Retribution'. The growled reply of the Captain to the dark-haired passenger immediately anticipates the storm which will bring an end to both their lives, though in different ways and at different times. The devil is at work in the storm and when the sick man lying on his wooden couch reads the inscription 'Batavia. Five hundred and ten', the way is already open for the gruesome ending of the poem.

When the storm comes, it comes not with colours changing across the sky but with loud noises, and the Captain is the first to feel its lethal power. The sick man, weakened by fever and his battle to live, can only submit to the waves, and only the passenger manages to survive among the wreckage, with the help of a soggy box which holds out little hope for him. The other man, whom he is shortly to condemn to a watery grave, tries to help him by calling out directions. His reward for that is that the passenger seizes him and wrenches him from his relative safety. The mercy that he pleads for, in his wretched state, is not forthcoming from the passenger whose one thought is for himself. The fate of the sick man is passed over, but the passenger is free, or so he thinks, when he is picked up by another ship, oblivious to the fact that those who seem to save him are pirates, and that his apparent rescue condemns him to death along with them.

It does not matter how he spent the three months which have passed as the second section opens: that is not the concern of the poet or the reader. What does matter is that the ship has come into land, where it has become a playground for the local lads, surrounded by the seals basking in the sun and watched by the young girls. This frivolous background is no more than that, however, for the drama which is about to be played out is focused on the impending outcome of the events which have not been described, and do not need to be: a trial presumably, and the sentences of death.

New characters now enter the scene, all unnamed like the main protagonists, except for Frei and Hessel, whom Droste-Hülshoff derives from historical accounts of robbers and their fates, and so endows the episode with a hint of authenticity. The focus is not, however, on them but on the dark Frenchman, for this story is at its base about him, the nameless passenger, and on him the poem focuses until its conclusion. The poem is not so much about a shipwreck, its victims and its survivors as about the selfish, perfidious nature of a human being, and the power of Fate - the Hand of God perhaps - to deliver his retribution.

The old woman who scoffs at his protestations of innocence tells all that we need to know of what has come to pass: that he has stood trial with those who saved him three months before and who have now disowned him and failed to corroborate his story. All the shabby acts of which we have heard culminate now as he stands on the gallows, condemned by his fellow men and judged by the God in whom he no longer believes. There is to be no mercy for him who showed no mercy to a fellow sufferer, and the final irony is pronounced by the inscription on the piece of wood.

Retribution

The Captain stands against the mast,
his telescope in his sunburnt hand.

He has his back to the dark-haired passenger.
After fleeting contemplation
the two men are standing like two pillars,
and the stranger asks: "What's that brewing in there?"
and the Captain answers with a growl
"The devil".

Then a sick man raises his damp forehead
from the ruins of the rotting girders.
The blue of the sky, the flickering of the sea:
all that torments his fevered brain.
He allows his gaze, ponderous and grim,
to scan the hard bolster,
and he reads the words inscribed there:
"Batavia. Five hundred and ten."

The cloud lifts. At midday the ship
groans on the crest of the waves,
hissing, howling, out of the barren depths.
The planks give way with a groan.
"Jesus, Mary! We are finished!"
The sailor is hurled from the mast.
There's a dull crack in every ear, and slowly
the structure comes away.

The sick man is still lying on the top,
clinging tightly to his plank.
Then come the surging waves,
and he is swept some distance
into the desolate sea.

Where the force of all his strength could not succeed,
the rigid cramp achieved, and like the narwhal
with its horn, he is propelled through the steaming waves.

How long does this last? He has no idea,
but then a ray of light strikes his eyeball,
and he is swimming with the wreckage
on the barren, glittering crystal.
The ship? The crew? They have sunk.
But no! There, upon the trail on the water,
he sees the passenger bobbing up and down
in a soggy little boat made of a wooden box.

Wretched chest! It will sink!
He forces his hoarse voice: "Keep straight!
My friend, you're heading towards the left",
and it floats closer and closer,
and closer and closer comes the wreckage,
like a seagull's nest blown away in the wind.
"Courage!" cries the sick swimmer.
"I think I can see land in the west."

Now the sterns of the ferries touch,
and he sees light in strange eyes,
and then suddenly he feels strong hands
and feels himself furiously torn from his seat.
"Mercy!" he cries. "I cannot fight." And he
clings on here and clutches there.
A hoarse cry, softened by the waves,
and the passenger is floating on the plank.

Then he has hurled himself with great force
and is rocking his way through the barren blue.
He can see the land dropping away like dusk descending,
vanishing in the grey light.
He swam on like this for a long time,
with the cry of the seagulls fluttering around him
and then a ship picked him up.
Victoria! Now he is free!

II
Three short months have passed
and the frigate is lying on the shore,
where at midday the seals bask in the sun
and lads clamber on board.
It's an adventure for the girls to watch from the distant reef,
for even in its wrecked state
the terrible pirate ship
does not frighten them.

And in front of the town there is wading,
burrowing away through the squeaking gravel,
where everyone is wanting to see
the notorious pirates die.
They have built the gallows close by the sea,
thrown together in desperate haste,
out of bits of rotten driftwood.
It looms threateningly across the dunes.

What a racket at the barriers!
Here comes Frei - and now Hessel!

Now they are bringing the black Frenchman,
who up to now has pleaded innocent.
"He says he swam here after a shipwreck",
scoffs one old woman. "Ah, what a cheek!
But no one spoke up for him,
the whole bunch against him."

The passenger, standing on the gallows.
hollow-eyed, his spirits broken,
pleads in a whisper with each robber:
"What is my innocent blood to you?
So I must die
because of the lies of that rabble?
Oh, may your souls rot!"
But the man in charge is dragging him away.

He sees the crowd split up and drift away -
he can hear the buzzing in the throng.
Now he knows that the might of heaven
is just a charade made up by his priests.
And when, with proud contempt,
he tries to stare up at the skies,
he reads in the wood of the gallows
"Batavia. Five hundred and ten".

The Sisters

This long ballad was written in Meersburg in that significant
winter of 1841-42 when, with Levin Schücking in residence as
librarian at the Castle, Droste Hülshoff was inspired to produce

lyric poetry of enormous power and emotion. This poem, the last of the so-called Meersburg ballads, belongs with these lyric poems and shares much with them. It was followed, when she returned to Westphalia in the autumn of 1842, by the powerful 'Familiar Spirit of the Horse-Dealer', and then, back in Meersburg, by her last, brief, sustained period of writing, which included some of her finest lyric poetry but never by anything remotely comparable in the realm of narrative.

By now it was perhaps less important where she wrote, whether in the Rüschhaus or far off in Meersburg, than that the inspiration of the thoughts she had evolved and was instantly evolving, and above all the impact of her friendship with Schücking, were deeply entrenched in her mind, and that her creative power, now at its peak, could turn equally to lyric and to narrative, with outstanding success and amazing versatility. Thus, while by no means belittling her earlier narrative verse, one can group together 'The Return of the Mother', 'The Founder', 'The Sisters' and 'The Familiar Spirit of the Horse-Dealer' when attempting to demonstrate her brilliance in this type of poetry, and, strangely, add to these the two poems - so different from one another and from any other poems of the same brief period - on Cologne Cathedral.

In the absence of firm evidence, one can sometimes only guess where Droste-Hülshoff found the material for her narrative poetry. We know that she gathered up ideas from many sources: her copious reading, historical events, anecdotes she had heard and kept in mind for future reference, folk tales, and, as in the case of 'The Jew's Beech', from contemporary reports that came to her notice. Whatever her original source, and even when there may have been no source at all outside her fertile imagination, she gave the material her highly individual treatment and made it her own.

It may be that the story that lies behind 'The Sisters' was something she had heard circulating in the neighbourhood. After all, the young boy who accompanies the huntsman as his gunsman at the end of the poem has obviously heard rumours and tells 'the awful tale in a whisper'. The place where the two men find themselves is known to be shunned by animals because it was there that 'they buried mad Gertrude from the Shore'. The idea sometimes suggested that there is an autobiographical element in the poem is surely less likely: Annette was close to her sister Jenny of course, but the intensity of emotion in this poem does not seem to reflect the relationship between them, which was one of affection and easy companionship, rather than the passionate interdependence amounting to a fusion of identities suggested here. One should perhaps go no further than to presume that she built on the idea of two sisters and that her imagination did the rest.

That is not to say, however, that the loneliness and despair of the poem do not, to some extent, reflect the experience she knew of loneliness: when her sister married and moved to Switzerland, leaving her very isolated in the family home, and later, with the realization that Schücking would soon be leaving Meersburg, followed by the deep depression she suffered once he had gone, and when the news came of his betrothal and marriage. These periods of her life are reflected in her letters, and in her poetry, but what Gertrude suffers in 'The Sisters' is something different: the sheer panic of loss coupled with her sense of having been responsible for her sister's disappearance and of having betrayed the trust of their dying mother. If there is indeed a touch of autobiography, it is perhaps to be found in

Droste-Hülshoff's very nature, the sense one has that, from childhood, she felt a deep loneliness, a feeling of being apart from others, and this in spite of her apparent sociability and commitment to the well-being of those around her. Her response to her early experience of love reveals her tendency to take upon herself the guilt for circumstances not always within her control and to brood upon them to a point where she withdrew into a deep depression and even sometimes feared for her own mental stability. It cannot be doubted that she understands the state of mind of Gertrude as the poem progresses to its terrible end.

The first two lines of 'The Sisters' establishes the mood of the poem: the decaying coffer and the beetle knocking inside it; the moon over the pine forest. The action of this poem, which is full of action, physical and emotional, from its beginning, is set against this background, and the repetition of these lines, almost verbatim but in the past tense, at the end of it, underline the inevitability of what has happened.

The first strophe tells us all we need to know of the circumstances of Gertrude's frenetic search: she has allowed her younger sister, whom her mother on her death bed had placed in her care, to go out alone, and now she cannot find her. Two factors are emphasised: Helen took with her 'the dogs', including the faithful Fidel who will play such an important part in the events of the future, and was heading towards the town, that alien place where, as time will reveal, though only in part, such awful things befell the young girl. This is as yet unknown to us, and for the time being, the concentration is on the early stages of the frenzied search which, we now learn, is taking place at night, when the moon plays tricks on the eyes, and sounds are distorted.

In her sheer panic, Gertrude takes refuge in the familiar

comforts of her life: the rosary she carries with her, and her appeal to the Virgin Mary and to God Himself. These strophes are reminiscent of passages in Droste-Hülshoff's lyric poetry of the same years, in which familiar sights and sounds are transformed into experiences which are unfamiliar and sometimes threatening (see, for example, 'The Boy in the Moor', 'Moon-Rise'). Side by side with these sensory experiences is the insight she shows into the reaction of this woman, the elder sister terrified and racked with guilt, in a state of wild panic, but only at the start of a search which will last for years and change her life forever, and lead ultimately to her death.

When she calls out the name of her sister, the only response is the bleak echo that comes to her, 'a sad and lonely sound' sent back home, to a home that the sisters will never enjoy again. Indeed, the home of their youth is never mentioned: presumably Gertrude never returns to it. Her environment from now on is unclear, moving as it does from the town where she is tossed about in the throng of people and believes she sees her sister disappearing into a stately mansion, and the lake where both sisters meet their end.

The other human beings who share in this first terrible night are ordinary people: the young mill-workers whose night is spent guarding the huge vat but who are constantly alerted to the cries they believe to come from some crazed ghost that haunts the forest with its lantern. Already Gertrude, the elder sister, has been transformed, and the German word for ghost, ('das Gespenst') with its neuter gender, suggests the decline of the woman from the human into the creature she will become. Just for a moment, at the end of this first section of the poem, some kind of humanity asserts itself, when another woman going about her business of collecting brushwood, chances on the ravaged, sleeping Gertrude. In the light of the morning, something of normality returns, but Gertrude's dreams are terrible dreams, and she will not be the same again.

Droste-Hülshoff's ability to convey contrasting moods is evident as the second section opens, and the noise of the town replaces the eerie silence of the night with its strange and threatening sounds. These new sounds are not pleasing sounds, but at least they are identifiable and associated with a range of identifiable individuals. However, they belong to their own world, and into this world steps a slender woman who belongs not in the Babel of the town but in the hills. Two features characterize her: that her eyes scan the ground, as though she were looking for something, which, as we know, she is, and that behind her trots a shaggy dog, with drooping ears, bewildered as she is herself. This must surely be Fidel, the faithful dog who joined her on the first, fateful night in response to her calls to her sister and who has still a major part to play in this tragic search.

How long the woman and the dog have been walking together is not known. Like so many details in this mysterious poem, we are not told, nor do we need to know. The central event of this second section is their progress now through the throng in the streets, and the perilous encounter with the cart and horses which causes her to leap across the gutter and catch her apron in the wheels of the cart. She manages to tear herself free, and with a torrent of abuse surely alien to the lady she is meant to be, she makes her way across the muddy street and finds herself standing by a chance, which is probably not a chance, in front of a grand mansion.

When she glimpses a purple dress disappearing through the

gate, she believes this must be her sister, but for the first time she doubts her sanity, and knows that the grief she has experienced is bringing her close to madness. The progress of this deranged state will occupy the whole of the poem now: the way is prepared for the mental disintegration which will lead to her desperate suicide. Only briefly, as the second section ends, does a moment of reason come to her when she tells herself that her sister could never be responsible for the wretched state of the faithful dog. Ten years will pass now, the first measure we are given of time, indeed the only indication ever supplied of the passage of time.

The two central figures are transformed: her black hair is now silvery grey, and the dog which bounded up to her in the forest when she called out her sister's name is now 'the limping spitz', inseparable from her as they walk their lonely way together. The only tangible insight we are given into her way of life is the strange reference to the honeycomb she carries, to be delivered to the captain of the ship in the harbour, and her anxiety that he may not give her even the small payment she might hope for. The implication that the years have brought her this material hardship is just one of the many details Droste-Hülshoff packs into this poem which is so rich in innuendo, but it passes and is replaced by the next significant happening, when the dog uncovers the body which the waves have deposited upon the shore.

Now so much is said in simple, powerful language: Gertrude is afraid, sensing as she does that her search is at an end; the unkempt dog, lame and whimpering, recognizes his mistress after all these years; and the corpse itself is terribly distorted. Droste-Hülshoff does not flinch from this stark discovery, any more than

Gertrude herself, who gently probes the body for the signs she knows she will find to confirm the identity of her long-lost sister.

What she does now restates the love that has kept her faithful to her search, and two sounds express her anguish at its dreadful end: the whimpering that links her so poignantly with the dog, but then, when the sailor unknowingly reveals the sordid story of the dead woman, 'the hollow cry' that she lets out before she collapses in the sand.

So much of the brilliance of Droste-Hülshoff is contained in this finale: the depth of her understanding of human emotions, but, above that, her capacity to write with extraordinary compactness to express them. Just as characteristic of Droste-Hülshoff's powers of narration is the way she now changes the mood, once more, for the final section. In it she distances her reader from the terrible tale she has unfolded by placing it in the mouth of a new and unnamed protagonist. The huntsman who takes over the narration begins in easy, almost casual, style, as he tells of a recent experience. Yet again it is the sounds which add to the description: the barking of the deer, the cracking in the undergrowth and the barely discernible sound of the woodworm beneath his feet. But then there is the movement of the deer as it slips away, alerted, he assumes, to their presence.

The chance mention by the young gunsman who is accompanying him reintroduces the name of Gertrude, but now with the two qualifying descriptions, which open up this final account of her end and her reputation. No doubt the local lad is very familiar with the story which he now relates of 'mad Gertrude from the Shore' and which fills the older man with fear. What he must now come to realize is that the knocking beneath his feet is coming from the coffer of mad Gertrude, condemned to be buried in the forest because she chose to take her own life in the waters of the lake that had claimed her sister.

What the people who saw her sail away and hurl herself from the reef do not know, the story has already told us. She never revealed when questioned who the strange drunken woman was whom the waves had deposited on the shore, although popular gossip held that she had searched for her until she found her, 'old and terribly distorted', 'mad and wild'. Rumour had it that she had been 'struck by evil' and had spoken 'questionable things' the boy prefers not to repeat, which was why they denied her proper burial but buried her in the undergrowth like the lost soul they judged her to be. It is left to the huntsman, a complete stranger who has chanced that way where no animal ventures to go, to pronounce the gentler judgement on Gertrude, or perhaps, we are meant to think, on both the sisters, since the elder sister sees in the waters of the lake the face of Helen, but also of herself. Both emerge as 'poor, hunted, anguished creatures', wronged by their fellowmen, and the cry of the huntsman for revenge is a rare judgement from Droste-Hülshoff who seldom expresses so clearly the unclear nature of human guilt and the need for expiation of guilt.

The Sisters

Softly the beetle knocks inside the decaying coffer.
The moon hangs over the pine trees.
"Jesus, Maria! Where can she be?
My fear is going to destroy me.
Helen, Helen! Why did I let you go alone
with the dogs into the town,

you poor child, whom our dying mother
so fervently entrusted to me?"

And Gertrude runs up the path again
and over the hill.
Here there is a ravine, and she listens on the slope.
A shrub: she shakes the branches.
It strikes eleven down below in the tower.
Gertrude kneels on the incline:
"You poor wretch! You abandoned mite!
Where can you be wandering about in the forest?"

And trembling she loosens the rosary
hanging from her belt.
Her eyes stare out in the murky glow,
as if dusk were breaking forth.
"Ave Maria - a light, a light!
She's coming. It's her lantern!
Oh God! It's just a shepherd's fire,
and now it's throwing out fluttering stars.

Our Father, who art in heaven,
hallow'd be Thy name" -
There's a noise on the slope. "Blessed Christ!"
There's the sound of breaking and cracking in the gorse.
and above it stretches a slender neck,
and two shining eyes stare out.
"Oh, God, it's just a hind,
and now she's making her way across the fern."

Gertrude climbs up the hill
and stands in the middle of the meadow.
There it is - are her ears deceiving her? -
A swift trot, quickly galloping steps.
And there's a chaotic circle leaping around her,
and the sparkle of delighted groaning.
"Fidel! Fidel!" she whispers softly,
and then she is sobbing and calling out "Helena!"

"Helena!" comes the echo from the cliff-face,
"Helena!" from the edge of the forest.
It was a sad and lonely sound
that the echo sent back home.
Down below in the ravine,
where the mill-wheel stands on guard,
the dusty lads at the huge vat have been listening out all night
to the crazed ghost in the pine forest.

They heard its shouting hour after hour,
saw the glimmer of its lantern.
and they made the sign of the cross on their breasts and their lips
whenever the light shimmered across the ravine.
And when the miller-woman was collecting brushwood
at the edge of the forest in the early morning
she found poor Gertrude in the grass,
jerking with fear in her dreams.

II

How the din of the market rolls through the alleyways!

What a jumble of noise and lightning!
The clown peers out over his booth
and shakes his jingling cap.
Carriages clatter, drinkers shout their hurrahs,
and girls shriek in the throng.
Barrel-organs pipe away, a labourer lets out a curse:
Oh! sounds worthy of Babel!

Then a woman steps out of the doorway of a shop,
a slim woman from the hills,
pushes against the jingling harlequin.
She has not been laughing, not been shrieking.
Her weary eyes search the ground
as though she has lost something,
and behind her trots a shaggy dog,
bewildered, with his ears drooping.

"Get back, you bold one!
Can you not see the cart,
The snorting brown horses?"
Already her nostrils are wet with moisture,
And she starts back in amazement,
and has slipped right over the gutter with a quick leap,
just as the clattering wheel touches her apron
as it whirls round.

Another moment - she staggers, turns pale,
and then suddenly glows bright red.
Oh look, how she coughs her way through the throng,
with her arms and her hands and her knees.

She rows her way through, turning this way and that,
giving forth a stream of abuse and curses like hailstones.
Her apron tears and flutters loose,
and floats away in the gulley.

Now she is standing in front of a stately mansion,
shoeless and covered in mud.
At that point the carriage comes to a standstill,
there the brown horses snort and snort, steaming like chimney-pots.
The barrier is open, and she can just glimpse
the fold of a dress, glowing purple,
disappearing in the gateway,
and a veil flapping in the breeze.

"Ah," whispers Gertrude. "What have I done?
In truth I have gone mad.
No consolation by day, no rest by night.
That can surely kill one's senses."
Then there is the sound of shouts and thuds coming down the stairs,
footsteps out of the gateway,
and, whimpering, her dog, the shaggy, pale dog,
tumbles down from the ramp.

"Yes," sighs Gertrude. "Now it is clear.
Alas: I have become a mad woman."
Reddening, she pushes her hair back
and straightens her dusty clothes.
"Yet how distinctly did I see her beloved face,
rising so clearly above the barrier!
But never in a million years
would she have beaten poor Fidel."

III

Ten years! And many a man who boldly shot
his sparkling glances all about him then
casts them firmly to the ground today,
and many a man has closed them altogether.
On the harbour wall a lady walks -
I think we must know her -
her hair once black, now silvery grey,
and her cheeks burning and hollow.

In a pot she carries a honeycomb,
melting in the heat of July,
and its bearer wipes the sweat from her brow
and calls to the limping spitz.
The man who placed the order, the captain of the ship,
sees her coming across the plank.
Will he bother to give her the meagre payment,
Gertrude wonders anxiously to herself.

But no: she sees him striding towards the shore
where the men are gathering.
He shakes his head and strokes his beard
and seems to be pointing towards the waves.
And look at the dog: he is scuffling at the ground.
"What are you looking for in the tracks,
Fidel, Fidel?" And the dog stumbles off,
howling like a wolf in a trap.

Merciful heaven! She is so afraid.

She wades through the burning sand
and again the wailing of the dog sounds out
so hollow from the shore.
Oh God! A drenched corpse among the pebbles,
a corpse with the eyes of a bull,
and the shaggy coat of the whimpering, lame dog
is creeping all over it.

Gertrude stands there, staring down,
her eyes more and more deranged,
then she bends down over the corpse
with a smile more and more befuddled.
She turns this way and that,
whispering with her jerking lips,
and before two minutes have passed,
she is kneeling prostrate on the ground.

She holds the swollen hand of the dead woman,
her hair full of shells and seaweed.
She takes hold of her dripping, ragged dress
and cleans the pebbles from her cheeks.
Then gently she pushes the cloth back,
just where the shoulders form their round shape.
Her gaze rests there, vacant, boring its way in,
as though she has found something.

Now she starts up, suddenly gets to her feet
and lets out a whimpering groan,
at the precise moment when the sailor spoke and said:
"That is blond Helen. Once upon a time she used to pass by
on the shore with drunken soldiers,

shouting her hurrahs,"
At that Gertrude uttered a hollow cry
and collapsed in the sand.

IV

I was standing recently by the lake, among the pine trees,
my gunsman at my side.
From the mountain slope the bold deer barked its call
and slipped away through the expanse of trees.
I heard its cracking sound so distinct and so close by,
just where the clearing was growing dark,
so that even the woodworm hammering away beneath my feet
disturbed me.

Then it leapt down. Probably the air was carrying
 our scent towards it.
"Sir", the lad said. "Across the ravine, to the left!
We must go towards the left.
No animal will come this way, where they buried
Mad Gertrude from the Shore.
I can clearly hear the woodworm
Knocking in her crumbled coffin."

I jumped to the side, frozen with fear.
It was as if I had committed some sin,
as the lad told the awful tale in a whisper:
How she searched
day and night
for the strange drunken woman

whom the faithless lake had brought to her,
lost in body and soul.
Was she of her blood? They did not know.
No amount of questioning penetrated her silence.
But the waves became calm, and then
one could see her face bent over the mirror
which showed her own image to her.
And then she whispered in confusion:
"How old she looks, how mad and wild,
and how terribly distorted !"

But when the storm stirred up the waves,
she was struck by evil,
and he would rather not say
what questionable things she said.
And so she ran away before the year's end -
they saw her from the ship as it sailed away against the wind -
towards the waves, where they are at their deepest,
and fell head-first from the reef.

"And so they buried her there in the undergrowth,
like a lost soul."
I remained silent and sent the lad away,
And broke a reed for myself from the grave.
"You poor, hunted, anguished creature!
How can humankind avenge you?"
Softly the beetle knocked inside the rotted shrine.
The moon hung over the pine trees.

CHAPTER VI

✤

THE REBUILDING OF COLOGNE CATHEDRAL: 'MEISTER GERHARD OF COLOGNE' AND 'THE CITY AND THE CATHEDRAL'

Annette von Droste Hülshoff spent some pleasant months between October 1825 and April 1826 in Cologne. After the catastrophic events of the summer of 1820, and the searing guilt she felt for the collapse of her friendship with Heinrich Straube and August von Arnswaldt, she had to a large extent withdrawn into depression and self-accusation and cut herself off from the social contacts she had cherished until that time. She was deeply embarrassed by what had happened, and, feeling that some members of her extended family had been complicit in the episode and subsequently blamed her for its outcome, she had deliberately withdrawn from them. The journey to the Rhineland, with her elder brother and his wife, and the gradual development of a new social circle, were welcome and thoroughly positive, and she soon found herself adapting to a very different life from the one she had been living in Münster. Her creative life benefited similarly, and she was able to work again with real commitment, notably on 'The Spiritual Year'.

Cologne had only relatively recently been emerging from its position as an occupied town during the closing years of the

Napoleonic Wars, and it must have represented for her a vibrant city with a surrounding landscape so different from her native Westphalia, and activity very different from the drawing-rooms of Münster. It is not impossible that when she describes Gertrude in 'The Sisters' encountering the bewildering melée in the streets of the town in her desperate search for her sister, she was recalling her first impressions of a city alien to her but offering new challenges at a significant time of her life. In Cologne she formed some important new friendships and connections, and she returned there for shorter visits later, by which time she was beginning to establish herself as a poet.

The letters from Annette to her mother and her sister speak of her excitement at this first major period away from home and in a totally new environment. She refers to a Christmas that was full of fun and novelty, to the Carnival celebrations in February, to balls and parties, but one of the most moving descriptions comes soon after her arrival there, in the middle of October. She describes seeing the great new steamer, the *Friedrich Wilhelm*, shortly after the naming ceremony, and of the impression made upon her by this magnificent ship: 'something enormously imposing, one can even say, terrifying', she writes, and goes on, in a letter longer and more detailed than many she wrote during those action-packed weeks, to speak of the noise it makes, 'as if it were about to take off into the air' (Letter to Therese von Droste-Hülshoff, 18 October 1825). It is like a machine from hell, she enthuses, and seems quite undeterred by all this, when she looks forward to making the five-hour trip to Koblenz. This ambition was to remain unfulfilled, however, until quite some time later.

Within a year, life was going to change for Annette and her

family, with the sudden death of her beloved father and the ensuing changes to all their lives, when her brother Werner and his family moved into Castle Hülshoff and she and her mother into the modest Rüschhaus in the countryside outside Münster, where she was to write some of her most powerful poetry.

One can hardly doubt the impact of this first visit to Cologne, and, with her powerful memory and habit of tucking away ideas and impressions, she almost certainly had it in mind when she wrote the first of two long poems, certainly not ballads in any technical sense, based on the project to complete the building of Cologne Cathedral . The great building which looms over the Rhine, as it did then, is the focus of the city, but what dominated at that time was the sense that it was unfinished, and that the great crane which all could see was testimony to a plan which had been stopped and started several times since the Middle Ages. It is, after all, the huge ambition which fills the mind of the Archbishop as he rides through the forest towards his assassination in her great poem of 1841 and it is again the thought which inspires the very different 'Master Gerhard of Cologne' of a little later that same year. In this rather charming poem, she turns to the legend of the medieval builder-architect credited with having planned in detail how to complete the building in his lifetime. Legend had it that he made a pact with the devil that he would not die until his work was done but that he died in a mysterious fall and his ghost went on to pace the building at night and climb up on the towering crane, awaiting the day when all would be set in motion for the fulfilment of his master plan. Droste-Hülshoff seems not to have thought so highly of this poem, which has its roots in the romanticism of her not so distant predecessors. She dismissed it as belonging with the ghost stories ('Spukgeschichten') at which, as we have seen, she excelled, and of the two poems she offered to Levin Schücking, it was the second that she valued more highly. What both together give to us, in an examination of the range of her poetry, is yet another example of the brilliance of this remarkable writer.

When, in late 1842, her thoughts turned to another poem on broadly the same subject, she was witnessing a bigger, nationwide campaign to forge ahead with a project which was to see Cologne Cathedral built in accordance with the lofty concepts of the past, to proclaim the status of a triumphant Prussia. Not first and foremost political in her leanings, Droste-Hülshoff, an intelligent woman who mixed socially with some of the thinkers of her generation and cannot have failed to form opinions on what she heard and saw, seized the opportunity to link two contemporary issues, the completion of Cologne Cathedral, and the restoration of Hamburg after the devastating fire of 1842, in a poem very different in its manner and its thrust.

Meister Gerhard of Cologne

The opening of this poem, with its description of the Rhine in the light of the full moon, is reminiscent of so much of Droste-Hülshoff's writing in its lyrical beauty and the evocation of sight and sound and fragrance, and in her use of metaphors. Night is personified, as is the great river, and over all that the city, Cologne herself, sleeping and dreaming.

The first four strophes have as their keynote dreams and dreaming: the river dreams, the forest dreams, the porter on the river-bank lies 'like a seal' and dreams. At the conclusion of the poem, Droste-Hülshoff asks: 'Have I been dreaming?' for this night-time vision, which she evokes on the basis of a legend current at that time and very familiar to her, has indeed the quality of a dream throughout, and central to it is the dream of the medieval master himself that his cherished plan will be fulfilled. Now, in her own age, the aspirations of a whole new generation are seen, in this poem, and in 'The City and the Cathedral', as a modern dream.

In the third strophe, the cathedral looms above the city as the product of an age-old dream, not only the hopes of the Middle Ages, but reminding those who see it, as she herself must have done many times during her stay in 1825-1826, of the centuries of history encompassed by the great building, left a magnificent stump for so long and always with the giant crane a reminder of a project unfulfilled. Against that background, so powerfully evoked, the small figure of Meister Gerhard emerges to dominate the poem as its single protagonist, as he makes his way through the huge building at night and leaves no shadow. Levin Schücking wrote to Droste-Hülshoff of his admiration for her description of this spectral vision, which was as beautiful as any she created in her more traditional 'ghost-stories': 'It is indeed incomparably lovely', he said.

It was in Schücking's own work 'Cologne Cathedral and its Completion' (1842) that this poem made its first appearance, although later, when they came to select poems for the 1844 edition, she wrote to him that she would rather sacrifice it than what she calls 'its rival', 'The City and the Cathedral', which she describes as one of her best poems (Letter of 17 January 1844). In the event, both were retained in that first big edition of her work, a testimony to their mutual respect, and to the soundness of his judgement. Interestingly, too, it was Schücking who added the subtitle 'Nocturne' ('Ein Notturno'), which perfectly sums up the mood of this poem and distinguishes it from the other 'ghost-stories' she had written at about the same time. It also demonstrates the sensitivity of Schücking, who, in his dealings with her, was not always noted for his sensitivity, but who clearly appreciated the gentle lyricism she achieves here.

Particularly striking is the way she evokes the atmosphere in the great building at night. Unfinished it may be, but the quality of the cathedral and many of its main features are recognizable in her description of this 'petrified forest of palm trees'. The great church is desolate, neglected over the centuries, and even desecrated during the years when it was inhabited by invading French soldiers, although now the only sign of life is the flowers and weeds which are thriving in the unfinished nave. Yet they are sleeping in the darkness, like the great buttresses a reminder of the Gothic origins of the building, and a stark reminder of plans never fulfilled.

The sound of the bell cuts through the silence, and the mist from the Rhine, so simply yet so vividly described in the very first line, seems to enter from outside and mark the arrival of the little figure of the Master, all in grey, which suddenly stands there. At first the figure is an 'it' as it makes its deliberate way, gliding around the familiar features of the building and applying the symbol of its profession, the measuring stick, from time to time, intent, as the skilled craftsman remains in death, with the details of his trade. By now the phantom has become a reality, a little man clenching his fist, as he mounts the crane which stands motionless, a tragic reminder of a cherished task left unfinished and a commitment left, unfulfilled, in the hands of another age.

Talk of setting about the task of completing the cathedral had been given new impetus by the discovery of some of the late thirteenth-century plans for its rebuilding and continuation. Sulpiz Boisserée, the eminent art collector and art historian, had gathered support for his campaign from some distinguished figures of the age, among them Goethe, and Friedrich Schlegel, and eventually even, crucially, Crown Prince Friedrich Wilhelm of Prussia, later Friedrich Wilhelm III. The project was seen in some quarters as a demonstration of gratitude for the liberation of Prussia at the end of the Napoleonic Wars, but also, more abstractly, it reflected the Romantic enthusiasm for the Middle Ages. At about the time of Droste-Hülshoff's two poems, these issues coalesced in some firm resolutions, and the beginning of construction became a reality and gained financial and political support, though not without reservations which she and Schücking undoubtedly discussed. 'The City and the Cathedral' clearly expresses her misgivings that religious and commercial considerations were becoming confused, and she knew that Schücking was on a somewhat different side from her in the debate and certainly, journalist that he was, expressed himself in a different way. She was aware that he might raise objections to the thought expressed in the poem just a few months later, and that he might find its almost polemical standpoints displeasing coming from her.

For the time being, in this gentle poem, what dominates is the devotion of the little man in the little grey hat, who presents himself in strident tones during his nocturnal perambulations as 'the spirit of years past' and urges his successors to wake up from their sleep and begin to work on the task he had had to leave behind. His cry is a spirited call to unity in a country only just on the brink of recognizing that its strength depends on the people acting together, and only when that recognition comes can he, the *Meister,* hand on his measuring stick. His zealous cry breaks off in mid-sentence, and in a rare moment of what, in Heine, one would term *Stimmungsbrechung* (abrupt change of mood), Droste-Hülshoff returns to the immediate present, and to a steam-boat puffing its way along the Rhine, just as she admired it so much when she first went to Cologne as a young woman. This, for the moment, is the essence of Germany, and her thoughts are only dreams.

Meister Gerhard of Cologne

Whenever in the gentle nights of the full moon
the mists lie across the Rhine
and silvery grey threads weave a fine veil
over the shrine of the saint,
the forest dreams, encircled in fragrance,
the dark, snakelike river dreams,
and, like a seal, the porter lies on the bank -
and dreams.

Night draws its deep, moist breath.
The grasses on the embankment tremble faintly
and a sepulchral exhalation
lies over the sleeping city.
She hears the lullaby of the waves,
the soft murmuring of the foam,

and old Cologne sinks deeper and deeper
into dream.

And where the grey Cathedral,
gigantic product of an age-old dream,
rises out of the sombre ruins of the power
which also flowed away like foam,
the beam has poured forth tremblingly
within the circle of the crimson disc
and sinks, melting away in a dream,
into the very depths.

How terrifying is it in the petrified palm-tree forest,
vast and desolate,
where thoughts slide down
like anacondas,
cold and heavy,
and the shadow rises bloody,
upon the bloody martyr of the disc,
like the soul hovering above the exiled body.

The light from the lamps has gone out,
and in the nave, half-closed, sleep flowers and weeds.
The dark-grey buttresses lean forward,
like naked reefs washed on the river bank,
here swelling towards the altar,
and there stretching upwards, elongated,
looping their heads round in an arch,
and slumbering on.

And more and more heavily it runs with stone,
knobbed pillars and shafts,
and in the rays of light it gains a hazy life.
But listen! There is a groaning in the tower, and ha!
the bell is sounding,
and the mist is rustling gently:
it jerks, it whirls about, it ruffles, and now
it is standing there.

Enfolded in a little cloak of mist,
a small grey cap, grey garment,
grey collar round grey neck,
the measuring tool in its ashen hand,
the ray of light passing trembling through its limbs,
as though in secret mourning,
yet no shadow falls upon the floor,
upon the wall.

The head moves from side to side,
silently the figure floats through the building.
Now look how it glides around the pillars,
and now it is going towards the foot of the organ,
and at every point it applies its measuring tool,
weaving up and down.
And gently the jerking of its limbs comes and goes,
like mist in the pine forest.

Was that the mighty breath of night?
Ah! Sighs echoing away into the distance,
a quavering sound. Sepulchral air wells up

and fills the whole deserted space
and at the gate the little man clenches his hand
in the direction of heaven,
then, gliding upwards on the gateway,
he stands upon the crane.

And he passes the hand that holds the measuring tool
across the sleeping shafts,
and their snake-like form begins to swell.
They bubble up as though only half-awake
and then a voice booms out,
a dull, echoing, distant din,
like thunder stretching forth in a dream,
from within the very depths of the clouds.

"I was responsible for this building.
I am the spirit of years past!
Alas! This dull, slumbering field is much worse than a bier.
Oh, when, when will the hour come,
when I may gaze upon this thing long buried?
You mighty River,
you home of mine:
when will you awake?

I am the watcher on the tower.
My cry is hieroglyphics from the rocks,
the blast of my horn the tempest of the ages,
but they are sleeping, sleeping, sleeping!
And they will go on sleeping,
until I hear the sound of chisels on the stonework,

185

and a thousand hands sound as one hand.
But I do not hear it.

And I cannot rest until I see the old crane moving
and I can place my faithful measuring tool
into a loyal right hand.
Then, when a single hand-clap sounds
throughout the land,
and all the pulses beat as one,
and all the many million drops are a single river - "
When in the East the silver banner

of the morning flutters
and, a vanished streak of mist,
the Master climbs up upon the crane,
with the clanking of the wheel and whistling,
and a steam-boat, a smoking monster,
makes its way foaming
along the Rhine, the blue Rhine -
Oh, German men and German women! Have I been dreaming?

The City and the Cathedral
A caricature of the most sacred

By the time Droste-Hülshoff wrote this second poem on the
rebuilding of Cologne Cathedral, another factor had entered the
situation and changed her perspective somewhat, and the style
of the poem completely. On 5 May 1842 a fire began in a house
in Hamburg and raged for five days before it could be brought
under control. The city, a vital centre of commerce for so long,

was devastated, and plans were quickly conceived to rebuild it, though it took 40 years to do so. Droste-Hülshoff was by no means alone in bringing the two projects together, but not everyone questioned the motives of those who called for restoration, of the cathedral on the one hand, and the city of Hamburg on the other, in the angry way she does.

There is a cynicism in this poem which surprises, but clearly she felt very deeply about the issue, and had undoubtedly discussed it with Levin Schücking and knew, when she sent him this second poem, so different from the first, that it would trouble him, even shock him perhaps, with the intensity of the emotions expressed. Although she knew that it might prove offensive (*anstößig* is the word she uses), she is prepared to defend her attitude and her deeply-held opinion that the two projects reflect an arrogance that she finds intensely objectionable, and to defend with uncharacteristic vigour the merits of 'The City and the Cathedral' which she so prizes. This time, it was she herself who gave the poem its subtitle, which she doubtless borrowed from the 1821 work of that name by the Norwegian-born scholar and philosopher-poet Henrik Steffens, who spent much of his life in Germany and was an influential thinker and writer of that earlier generation. It aptly expresses, as did his lengthy treatise which contained some disparaging references to the proposed rebuilding of the cathedral, her sense of the conflict between religious thought and blatant material considerations.

When she told Schücking that she was not expressing herself against the rebuilding of the cathedral, only against the aggressive materialism which was attaching to it, she was entirely truthful, and the same was true of her attitude to the rebuilding of Hamburg. Indeed, the first two strophes speak of the money that was pouring in to support both projects, and she does not detract from the generosity of those who give, irrespective of their own means. What she laments is the obsession with material things which replaces the concern for the spiritual. Where is Jehovah in all this, she asks, and where His teachings? She misses the ordinary human emotions, of compassion and, above all, of humility. When people present what they are doing as regard for their nation, they risk raising their achievements to the kind of sinful pride that brought about the fall of Rome. This is an unmistakable warning, yet, fair and balanced as she always is, Droste-Hülshoff ends on a conciliatory note: she does not deprecate the urge to build and to rebuild, for buildings have their part to play in the future, and the single examples she takes of the Colosseum and Trajan's column speak of the glory of an earlier age, though the shallow aspirations to worldly fame may have passed away.

This, after all, is the woman who hoped that her work would be read long after her death and sought neither material reward nor critical acclaim. Indeed, both were long denied her and her alarm at what she seems in this remarkable poem to see as the dangerous distortion of proper values in a nation obsessed by its presentation of itself leads one to ponder again what path she might have taken, personally and as a great artist, and what different part she might have played in the future sadly not granted to her.

The City and the Cathedral

The Cathedral! The Cathedral, the German Cathedral!

Who will help us build Cologne Cathedral?
Thus from far and near does the river of the ages
thunder through German lands.
There's a procession, there's a noise,
like a mighty movement of the waves.
Who can count the legion of hands
in which a sacrificial coin glints?
And who the melodies which the echo of this cry
already completes?

And again the sound comes from the banks of the Elbe:
"The city! The city! The German port!"
And again from land to land progresses
the clinking of gifts offered.
The ships arrive one mast after another.
The palace rains down gold.
He who was never granted a roof of his own
constructs a vault over the needs of others.
And he whose own fire has never burnt
shares his crust soaked in sweat.

When the strength of an entire nation
raises its spear like this,
shaft against shaft,
for the sanctity of its God,
who would not have a burning desire for this finest fame?
And whose blood would not course through his veins
like fire, when the sweat of a whole nation
pours down like noble rain,
until a sheaf of corn ripens on the hot, ashen steppe
for many thousand people?

They think a whole nation has descended overnight
from saints,
that ancient German loyalty has woken again
in its oak coffin.
Oh, noble unity, if you indeed are one,
who then would be more worthy of a halo,
of a garland, than you,
you blessed one on German soil?
In your alliance you would bear the golden key
to heaven's treasure trove.

Come on, you warriors, then, come on,
you worthy band of champions of the Cross.
Give me your emblems then,
and your noble battle-cry!
Listen! That was the sailor's pipe sounding out
its harsh whistle from the nearby ship.
Countless banners were raised there,
a cantata hummed, a poem said.
Only the brown colour of humility was missing ,
and I did not hear the name Jehovah.

Where, Lord, is Thy legion
which on its knees is building at the altar?
And where, where, Thy Samaritan who melts
his tears in wounds?
Ah, whatever I have asked and listened for,
the German river has brought roaring unto me:
the German city, the German cathedral,
a monument, a league of commerce,

and over it I saw like a phantom
fading away the writings of Jehovah.

And someone who has barked at heaven
never trembled at any hell,
has placed himself upon the crane
which lifts the ramparts of his Babel.[1]
And someone who has never honoured a human bond,
has never burdened himself with any pain,
sends flooding from the coffer of his breast
a stream of inexpressible emotions,
and on the banks of the Elbe, on the green Rhine,
his heart receives its accolade.

Woe to you, who have mocked the angry God
on His own threshold,
who, like perjurers in playful scorn,
have raised your hands before the altar!
He is the Lord, and what He asks for,
lion and crocodile achieve.
So, go on building, build the temple,
build with earthly thoughts the holy place,
so that your better grandson may pray there
for your soul!

Do you know the Cathedral that strives
upwards, invisibly, with its thousand columns?
It rises where a faithful congregation
humbly lifts its arms.
Do you know the invisible city

with its thousand open harbours,
where your precious silver rattles?
It is the league of the Samaritans
where right hand grasps right hand,
and left knows nothing of it.

Oh, He who knows all, knows also
the barren dwelling of your soul.
Build store-houses and monuments,
but leave His name out of it!
He is no sand that scatters glittering dust,
no steam-wheel driving ships.
He is no false banner that the prodigal son
stole from the sea,
no password which smuggles the spy into the camp
to perpetrate his treachery.

Build, build! Around your memorial
sighs pious and true are uttered even so.
Build, beside your store-house the needy
will nevertheless be refreshed.
Can the battlements of your Babel
stamp you as a nation of the world?
Behold the deserts of Palmyra [2)]
where the shy antelope hovers!
Behold the city where the Colosseum rises
like a monster!

The strength of an arm does not kill
the worm that labours secretly,

the cold and naked graveyard worm,
nor the mad tempest of your songs.
A chaste and pious nation is strong,
yet sin consumes the marrow of the land.
That sin - oh Rome! - slowly devoured you
on your glorious path.
Trajan's column is standing to this day,
and his crowns have turned to dust![3]

[1]*Genesis 11,1-9*

[2] The beautiful city of Palmyra was a centre of commerce and culture much favoured for many decades as an influential Roman province, remote in the Syrian desert. Its special status when it was granted independence from Rome led to rebellion and its ultimate destruction by the Emperor Aurelian in 272 AD.

[3]The column erected in recognition of the conquest of Dacia in 113 AD by the Emperor Trajan is still standing in Rome, though the reason for it may be forgotten, along with the many other exploits of the man known as 'the best ruler' ('princeps optimus').

CHAPTER VII

※

THE FAMILIAR SPIRIT OF THE HORSE-DEALER

The last long poem that Droste-Hülshoff wrote is this retelling of a story told by the Grimm brothers (Berlin 1816), and it can aptly serve to represent the culmination of her narrative poetry. She wrote it in the autumn of 1842, in one of her longer periods at the Rüschhaus in her last years, and at a time of great personal significance. Her close relationship with Levin Schücking had not yet suffered its final break, but he had left her in Meersburg when her poetic genius was at a peak and she had produced many of her great lyric poems under his inspiration and with the challenge of a wager between them. The coming years would see his marriage and the deep depression that ensued when she had to accept that they would never be so close again, but she also came to see that, for all the significance she attached to him, she was by now sufficiently secure in her vocation and could write with a new and fruitful independence.

By 1844 they would have collaborated on the first proper edition of her work, achieved by correspondence for the most part. The letters that passed between them at this time reflect his respect for her both as a person and as a poetic genius, but, above all and despite her physical frailty, her own growing sense of freedom. Even the deep hurt he caused her when, in 1846, he published his novel *Die Ritterbürtigen* ('The Gentility'), and she felt he had betrayed her by revealing traits of the aristocracy which she had confided to him at the time of their intimate friendship, could not in the long run detract from the gratitude she felt for the part he had played in the realization of her true creative ability. Moreover, it is to Schücking that we owe the growth of her posthumous reputation, the personal details that probably only he could have revealed and the understanding of her as a human being, and the first complete editions of her work after her death.

It is interesting that she apparently told him of this long ballad-like poem only when it was finished, at the end of 1842, and added that she liked it very much (letter dated 27.12.42), a considerable departure, since she had for several years kept him informed of her work and deferred to him frequently. This very fact speaks of her awareness that she could stand alone now, but it also almost certainly says much for her relationship with the poem itself, which, in the context of the present volume, can appropriately be seen as the peak of her achievement as a brilliant and distinctive writer of narrative poetry.

There are some important factors which distinguish 'The Familiar Spirit of the Horse-Dealer' from the other poems which accompany it here and make it an appropriate poem on which to conclude.

The form is unique: it contains seven cantos of unequal length, and the strophes consist of four long lines, followed by two short lines; the metre is consistently iambic. If it resembles anything, it is perhaps the medieval German epics which she heard in the household of her brother-in-law, Count Joseph von

Lassberg, a renowned medievalist and proud collector of manuscripts, including one of the most significant manuscripts of the *Nibelungenlied*. It is not impossible that, although Droste-Hülshoff did not share his enthusiasm for older German literature, she did appreciate the impact of the recitations with which he entertained his guests in the evenings at Meersburg Castle and borrowed some features for 'The Familiar Spirit of the Horse-Dealer', which was clearly very important to her and merited a form which distinguished it from everything else that she had written. She was not sure how to describe it, calling it a 'longer poem' in her first reference to Schücking, but then deciding it was a ballad, although, for the 1844 edition of her works, she insisted that it should be set apart from others to which she accorded that term and stand very much on its own.

That, indeed, is what this remarkable poem does do, but it belongs also with her other narratives in verse, those which precede it in this volume, and with the 'verse-epics' of her earlier years ('The Battle at Loener Bruch','The Hospice on the Great St Bernhard Pass' and 'The Doctor's Legacy') which had found their way, as a major contribution, into the first edition of her existing works, in 1838. Nor can one talk about 'The Familiar Spirit of the Horse-Dealer' without referring to 'The Jew's Beech', the *Novelle* for which she is most famous.

When one thinks of what she achieved with this poem, one must surely be drawn to the famous quotation by Goethe, who, with Schiller, had designated 1797 - strangely, the year of Droste-Hülshoff's birth - their 'ballad-year' and set about the task of composing some of the most famous ballads in the German language. What he wrote, many years later in his essay 'On Art and Antiquity' (1821), reflected his admiration for the ballad as a genre which he called the 'primordial egg of literature' ('das Urei der Literatur'), combining lyric, epic and dramatic qualities into a single whole. Droste-Hülshoff's last long narrative poem has all those qualities, and it merits a special place in her oeuvre.

By the time she came to write it, she was confident of her creative strengths and surer than ever of her goals. It is probably for this reason that she appends, for the first and only time, a long and detailed reference to her source. If one compares the account in the 'German Legend' of the Brothers Grimm, and considers the changes she made and the different emphasis, one can arrive at a better understanding of the message of the poem, and a truer assessment of its place in her work.

* * *

The story as related by the Brothers Grimm begins with a description of the familiar spirit itself, a creature not quite a spider, not quite a scorpion, which squirms around incessantly in a little sealed bottle. Anyone who purchases this will experience abundant good fortune, popularity among his friends but fear from his enemies. It will protect him from arrest and imprisonment and always bring him strength in battle. But the man who keeps it until his death must go with it to hell, and if, to avoid this, he lays it down at any point, it will always find its way back to him. This is what happened to a soldier who bought it and then, recognizing its properties, hurled it at the feet of its former owner and hastened away, only to find it waiting for him when he returned home. Even when he tried to throw it into the Danube, it returned to him.

With this background, the account focuses on a horse-dealer from Augsburg and his driver, who were approaching another famous German town. At this point bad luck began to befall him: he lost eight horses in just a few days. When he lamented his ill-fortune, another driver tried to console him by advising him to go to a certain house and ask for the 'Society' ('Gesellschaft'). When he followed the directions he came upon the house, where some old men were sitting at a table. They appeared to know him by name and provided him with a little box. If he kept this with him, they told him, he would immediately know prosperity and achieve all he desired. There was, however, one condition: he should never attempt to open the box. They declined his offer of payment but required him to write his name in a large book: his hand was guided as he did this.

Arriving back at his home, the horse-dealer found a leather pouch containing three hundred talers, and this was only the first of his sudden material gains. He did not need to commit murder or theft to acquire all this new wealth, but when his wife asked how he had come by it, she was horrified and urged him to return the box, which was clearly something evil. The servant he dispatched to the house to deliver it, however, returned with the news that the 'Society' had vanished without trace. His wife, determined to rid themselves of this evil, secretly opened the box and released a black fly which flew off. The couple were left with nothing but misfortune in place of their earlier prosperity: their horses either died or were stolen, their corn rotted, their house was burnt to the ground on three occasions. The husband fell into debt and poverty, and in despair he killed his wife with a knife and shot himself in the head.

This dark story, so the account in Grimm relates, appears in many places and with different or additional features, some of which, clearly, Droste-Hülshoff incorporates into her own retelling of the original legend. The creature makes a strange buzzing noise as it moves constantly about, and this alienates those who hear it and suspect some strange magic afoot. Black in daylight, it emits a phosphorous glow at night. Most significantly, she will have learnt from her reading, if the owner permits himself a pious thought, or prays, or enters a church, one of the appendages of the creature can penetrate the glass of the bottle it may be in in that version of the story and deliver a sharp sting that deprives him of his strength. All that is left behind to indicate that it was once in a certain place is loss and ruin and corruption.

* * *

It is not difficult to see that this treasure- trove of details as supplied by the Brothers Grimm provided Droste-Hülshoff with a mass of features, many of which are identifiable in her poem, albeit sometimes changed or employed at different stages of her narrative. More important, however, is what she adds from her own fertile imagination, and for the message of her poem, which is obviously different from the relatively simple message of any legend.

Her horse-dealer is alone: no wife intervenes to change the course of events, and, even more significant than that, he makes his lonely journey alone, towards the conclusion which Droste-Hülshoff provides, and in doing so gives this great poem its essentially spiritual message of redemption and ultimate salvation. That, if we return to Goethe's 'Urei', is what gives it a quality which one may well describe as 'epic' in its scope and grandeur, and its capacity to move the reader. The horse-dealer makes his way through so many diverse experiences: his tender grief at the death of a much-loved horse, the temptation to seek to restore his fortune when he races desperately through the wintry night to the house where he makes the terrible commitment which, though not described in any detail, dictates the whole of the remainder of his life, and his tragic end. His breathless attempt to rid himself of the spirit which now attaches to him is related with all Droste-Hülshoff's acute sense of natural phenomena but can only culminate in the predictable knowledge that escape is impossible. In human terms he is an outcast, and the devastating fire destroys all that he valued in material things. From now on his life is one of loneliness and exclusion, until he comes to the understanding of a salvation which transcends everything he has ever experienced. His death returns him to where he started, beneath the linden tree of his childhood and in the love of the God he has sometimes rejected as he clings to a perverted set of priorities. Somehow Droste-Hülshoff manages to convey all this in brilliantly diverse scenes, with an extraordinary variation in the pace of her narrative, as this tragic figure comes at last to recognize that the evil he has espoused can be destroyed by the ultimate expression of good. His frenetic, epic struggle ends in peace.

There are so many moments of drama in the events which befall this tragic figure, and also of lyricism in the often delicate descriptions of the natural setting and of the overwhelming emotions contained here. It is the coalescence of all these qualities which makes her last great piece of narrative an eloquent expression of thoughts and ideas, and of poetic genius which have been evident throughout her work but combine to bring it to a splendid culmination. After this, the ailing poet continued to write, of course, producing much of her finest lyric poetry, concluding her spiritual cycle which, for some critics, is central to her achievement, writing occasional poems for the delight of her nearest and dearest, and numerous letters which touch on her deepest emotions and occasionally her thoughts on what she must have known to be her impending death.

In transforming the Grimms' legend as she does here, she reveals once more her extraordinary power as a poet, and as a human being. Self-accusing and burdened with guilt and a sense of responsibility, she nevertheless seems here to allow herself the privilege of release and hope. When she returns the wretched horse-dealer to the quiet meadow of his childhood and has the labourer cutting the grass push him in a wheelbarrow to the mortuary, she is making a huge statement at the end of a huge poem. This man has found a way to redeem himself, but that way is through the mercy of God. He is restored to the society that has shunned him for so long, from which he has alienated himself by avarice and obstinacy, and society admits him to its ranks when he is buried, not like Friedrich Mergel, on a carrion heap, but in a proper grave, and paid for by the parish. That is the judgement of the world, but, as his body is transported at his funeral, the church bell chimes, and above his grave are the angel's wings. He is beyond the reach of the dragon's claw which figures so powerfully on the grave: the evil that he sought and found and through which he endured such suffering is banished by the love of the Child in the arms of the Madonna, and by God's grace.

The Familiar Spirit of the Horse-Dealer

Thus he has tormented himself in vain, in vain has sold the
noble spot

where stands his childhood linden tree and the death-bed
of his parents.

In vain he many a day has sucked in the frost-laden breath,

in his frozen hand the rein crackling with the covering of snow,

at sunrise and at sunset,

and all for a crust of honest bread.

The horse-dealer kneels on the paving stones and strokes the
horse's fevered flanks.

From the bars of the balcony the light casts wild and moving
shadows.

By God, it is alive - a flash in its eyes! It shudders, trembles,
this way and that,

then stretches out, the nostrils heaving, forced on by the wild cry,

and out of its limbs swirls dampness,

the final battle of the warmth of life.

The dealer kneels and goes on stroking, not wishing to
trust his eyes,

and swelling upwards into his eyelids is the bitter foaming
of a man's tears.

Gently he reaches for the cover and lays it round the flanks of the animal.

Then he lets the light of the lantern stroke the tense sinews.

It is over, no breath,

and already the steam from the horse's flanks is drifting away.

He raises himself from the ground and stands there, this bowed-down man of sorrow,

and slowly he supports his forehead in the hollow of his hand.

What was today? What will be tomorrow? How could he think of this?

And he could feel the snake of despair run coldly down towards his heart.

What was? What is? He starts up,

a rustling sound close to his ear.

And calmly weighing in his hand the bridle and the rein of the dead horse, is a man

leaning against the next stall with oats and currycomb.

It is the burly carrier who drives the heavy limbs through frost and dust.

His broad floppy hat is drooping down the back of his thick neck,

and his grey-lashed eyes

are glinting calmly at the horse-dealer.

"Sir," he begins. "I am sorry for you. You have lost a fine beast,

But I know another one, as like to it as two corals on a rosary.

I can give you the name of the place, the house, and you can have it for two hundred guilder.

I also know a gentleman who would give half his inheritance to have it."

The dealer listens and stammers out:

"I am a very poor man."

"What, your splendid pair gone? The ones I saw at Eastertide

stamping their hooves so eagerly on the pavement? Then you are really to be pitied.

That brown of yours with the star on its forehead, that knelt before the ladies?

Oh no! Your white one with sparks spurting out of its nostrils?"

The dealer has turned away,

tugging at the rein, clenching his fist.

And the floppy hat stands there, deep in thought, assessing the wood of the coffer with a firm gaze.

"Sir", he whispers. "Get your hand on some smooth pistoles[1)]

The hour is passing. The moon is waxing, soon it will be the end of the year.

Have you never in your travels heard of the *Society*? "

The dealer looks around him in confusion

and murmurs "The *Society?*"

"Yes, which has helped many a man out of trouble

and takes not a penny in interest, just two words on a sheet of
white paper,

and which, even if you live to be a hundred, will never embarrass
you with any reminder.

You don't know it! don't know it? That's certainly a surprise to
me."

The dealer listens, without a word,

and the other man goes on:

"Listen, when on New Year's Eve the moon mounts up
unchecked,

and its light casts no shadow on a tree, a roof; when the banners
on the towers are silvery,

go to the sluice-gate, with the river on your right, the pine-trees
to your left,

take no notice of anyone you meet, don't bother if anyone
greets you,

and behind the churchyard there's a house.

It looks a bit deserted,

the legacy of a dead usurer, over which seven scoundrels are viciously fighting.

Inside a pale light flickers - you will certainly not be able to see it from a distance -

once a year on this night - otherwise the door and the gate are barricaded - and

it burns in a room at the back of the house where the *Society* meets.

You'll find them there until the cock crows."

The dealer turns and goes.

He sways across the yard as though drunk, sways into the colourful hallway.

The clash of cans, the shouting, it seems as if the roof were falling in.

And with a sigh he loosens his leather purse from his belt,

and full of apprehension reveals his meagre means, bit by bit.

Then he jumps up and the sound of his spurs

clinks defiantly across the courtyard.

But, however much he may call, may whistle, the stable is empty,

and only out of the hay-ricks a jumble of hay hangs like tousled hair,

and underneath steam heaps of straw.

Only the damp wick of the lantern throws little flames upwards with a slight crackle and casts a strange darting light on the horses lying there.

And in the window stands the moon's pale majesty.

[1])Pistoles were ancient gold coins, originally from Spain

II

This is what I call a winter's night! The corpse of the year!

May heaven have mercy on anyone whom necessity forces over these shiny paths!

They shimmer like a snake in the white sand of the Pyramids,

and above them hangs a sepulchral light, the moon on an invisible ribbon.

The air is filled with tiny sparks, and it draws the sighs of death towards it

and sends them whirling upwards.

Never, as long as man can recollect, has New Year's Eve poured itself forth so sharply.

The day has scattered snowflakes, and the evening covered them with glass.

In the farmsteads doves and chickens hunch groaning on their branches.

The dog howls in his haystack and feels the worm twitching in his brain.

During this night the ice has added

two spans to the river.

At the gate the watchman stands frozen stiff and breathes on his ice-cold fingers.

"Who's there?" "A friend!" and quickly he trudges along the stone wall of the bridge.

The recruit watches him swaying like a mast in the water:

"The man is either drunk or mad", he thinks and stands deep in thought for a little while,

crosses himself, pulls out his watch

and leans against his sentry-box.

The horse-dealer marches off into open country. He takes a breath and looks up.

Not the smallest cloud hangs in the immense edifice of the dark blue dome up there.

He turns and sees the town lying like a mass of mist, and over it,

on St Thomas's Tower, the shimmering weather-vane is waving.

He pulls his coat about his face

and strides off in the moonlight,

What's that across the way? Someone, a man, in a thin canvas tunic.

The dealer gives a start, but does not hesitate, though to be sure he sees the old man's sparse hair, his bald patch glinting in the snow as he strides past him,

and it is as though a thousand ropes were pulling him down, to the side of him.

He has clenched his fist against his heart.

Then onwards, on! No stopping!

The clods crunch beneath his feet and seem to be accusing him with their whimpering,

and the air to be bringing its death-rattle towards him with its hoarse breath.

In the icy pine forest a wayward life whirrs and clinks,

and the breath from his own throat surrounds him with specks of dusty sparks.

On, on! The die is cast!

Lost, or boldly won!

Then there is a sound like a little bell from afar, and then a little light comes floating

along the shiny, snaking path, has climbed up the curve of the hill.

The little bell whirrs, the little flame wavers, dark figures move about.

A priest bearing the sacrament is coming towards the bewildered man, and as it passes him

the monk lifts the host in blessing.

The dealer shivers in fear and it seems as though lead weights were tearing at his knees,

but onwards, on! And he allows the angel of mercy to pass him by.

Again he shudders: a crack! The surface of the stream trembles as it splits,

a blast of wind passes through the tops of the pine-trees, and the little crystal sticks tinkle.

Then he steps out towards the cemetery,

and in front of him is the deserted house.

He stares at it - a gloomy building, with sloping gable, iron staves and rows of nails

hanging like rusty teeth from the open gate.

The dealer hesitates, then, as cautiously as a fox in a gale, slips round the walls.

Does it not seem as though a light were burning inside?

He shakes himself, steps inside

and stands alone in the gloomy passageway.

He taps on the wall, turns round. There is a light flickering through the slit in the door.

Softly he bends towards the crack, listening, holding his deep breath.

No noise, no clearing of the throat, only the sound of a quill being moved firmly along,

and a trickling sound, like sand falling like dust through narrow rills onto the attic floor.

Gently he takes hold of the handle,

gently he knocks and opens the door.

III

How peacefully do the silent, humble people sleep in the bowels of the earth!

At last a pillow after hard straw, at last a harbour after a bitter journey!

The low hills rise barely visible above the bulging snow,

but the Angel of God knows them well and he stretches out his wings to protect them,

towards the little crosses which, stake upon stake,

stand in rows around the marble block.

The dragon creeps upon the plinth and seems to be clawing its way down to the ground,

towards the dead usurer beneath the stone, felled by his own criminal hand.

To be sure, gold gained for him an honourable grave beneath the cemetery wall,

but above it St Michael brandishes his flaming sword in anger and in grief.

Silvery grey, a nocturnal vision,

the judgement in stone is standing there.

From the deserted house, once his, where bloody tears have flowed,

a strange dawning light has poured down onto the marble stone.

It is as if the monument were trembling and swaying at a touch,

as if in the snow a hand were winding its way upwards towards the debtor:

he comes, he's approaching, the gate creaks.

He leans against the stone.

Pale as the marble above him, and dark as the cross by his side,

with drops of thawed frost sliding down from his forehead and his eyelids, like tears.

What he has suffered in this night, or whatever sins he may have perpetrated,

he has never complained of it to anyone, or explained to anyone remorsefully.

He stares into the darkness, as one does stare,

thoughtless and empty.

It seems to him as if he can still feel the hand that guided his quill,

as if he can feel the prick of the needle that released the flow of his blood, and trembling slightly he gropes for his belt - can you not hear a clinking sound,

much louder than the ticking of a clock, much gentler than the jangling of a bangle?

Oh, his home, silently covered in foliage!

Oh, his father's grey head!

Unaware, he presses his forehead against the Angel's knee, clenches his fist.

He hears the bells of the dead nags slipping through the walls of pine-trees.

Opposite him on the horizon slide black streaks of cloud.

The folds of the funeral cloth fall gently onto the coffin, careless as an idle hand.

He rubs his eye, straightens up,

and gazes up towards the vaults of the sky.

Still the lamp of the moon hangs brightly from the gold embroidered dome.

Like a double spear the cross still gleams from the tower of the church of St Thomas.

It is not yet the hour when the cock shakes itself on its perch.

Oh, quick, quick! before the last grain of sand has run through the clock.

He turns, then - listen! - a sound,

and then another, heavy and afraid.

And by the twelfth stroke the cloak of cloud has stretched out,

spreading higher and higher, enormously high, above the cupola of the sky,

and listen! a drawn-out cry, the midnight lamentation of the cock.

At that very moment the light on the sarcophagus quivers and goes out,

and Angel, dragon, flaming sword

have all returned into the barren night.

IV

Ho! The clinking of glasses and merry singing and "Hurrah, hurrah!" resounds through the windows.

The 'Golden Lion' is rocking with the din, the lads are scattering in all directions,

and shoving one another, and fighting to catch the flying sweetmeats.

A glass, a fruit, even a purse, were all speared on the point of a shield,

and the greedy little beasts sting their way,

yelling, towards the pole.

Then through the balcony door clatters a man with a whip and iron spurs,

and after him another, bottle in his hand, lost in the bliss of intoxication.

"You rabble", calls the first. "Stop! I'll teach you to steal purses!"

"Come on, lads, come on!" adds the other man. "That's my pear: who can pluck it?

I'll dub him this very day, I, Hans von Spaa,

as Knight of the Land of Scoundrels"

"Just think", says the first man. "What's that about thinking? Did I think

when your yellowy horse collapsed at the fountain like a wounded bull?

Did I think of paying, sir? Oh, your cattle! Three hundred kroner?"

His voice breaks in drunken misery. "May the devil reward you!" he sobs.

And he turns the corkscrew in the bottle.

The dealer mutters gloomily

and turns to go. "Hey, hello! Stop!" comes the cry from behind him." Don't you move an inch!

Cheers for your little gallows man! Cheers for your smokey little pal!

And cheers again, and three times cheers! The little mandrake, little hat, as far as I'm concerned

May it go on laying golden eggs for you, and dead skins for other people."

The dealer smiles, ashen-faced

and strolls off into the hall whistling.

Another couple of minutes and you can see the alley mob making way for him

as he slinks along the rows of houses as shyly as a wild animal when cornered.

Thus does no drinker with all his wits about him and full of zest slink away from the feast.

Thus does no free heart bestow a greeting. Such sombre questions do not sit upon an unlined brow.

People assume a rascal is making for the gate now,

chased by believers.

 Only when the pine trees stare all about him, and their needles rustle beneath his feet

does he slow down his pace and stand, bowed over, listening, listening.

No lover listens so attentively to the sound of the bell that summons him to love,

no sick man to the footsteps of the priest who brings him forgiveness with the sacrament.

A reprobate may listen thus

to the striking of his final hour.

The forest lies slumbering in the heat of the sun in waves of perfume,

and resin trickles from the pine needles, as tears trickle from the eyelids of the sleeper.

The sun-drenched cliff is nodding, and the birds are dreaming of their song.

The squirrel lies curled up, his bushy tail flicked over him like a fringe.

White foam on every needle

sprays forth the breath of turpentine.

Through the branches the rays of sunlight penetrate the wavy hair of the listener

which glimmers in the dark mass like the fiery sparks of a sea-monster.

He stands there, listening; he listens, standing there. Can you not hear a faint sound,

as when grains of sand spurt on to the loft-floor through narrow rills?

It is such a sharp sound, and so penetrating,

like the whetting of the scythe upon a stone.

The dealer straightens up, he sighs, then pushes on towards the middle of the forest.

His spurs clink against the hideous toadstools, and blisters swell beneath his feet.

Here weeds and tangled reeds abound, wormlike creatures cling to every stem;

a mass of insects squirms up and down in the steaming moss,

and hissing, with its swollen spine,

the lizard heads for a hollow trunk.

The wanderer tears at the weeds, and breaks down the blackberry hedges as he rages through them,

until, sideways through the spear-like reeds, the inky darkness of the pond is glimmering,

a desolate bowl soaked as it were in the mulch of sulphurous asphalt.

Among the slimy threads and in the allium squirm long-legged, fluffy grubs,

and stale reflections,

blue and green, pass over like rainbows.

In the middle of all this stares out a dark patch, the pupil of a giant's eye,

and there the water-lily rises up, listening for every footstep in the silence.

Whoever it was she lured here with her radiance had sung his last
song.

For three days they searched in vain for the child, among the
weeds and vegetation,

where now leaches and water-spiders

feast on his pallid limbs.

The horse-dealer stands, arms folded, staring with dark
countenance into the pool.

His hair full of leaves and burrs sticks out strangely over the brim
of his hat

and like a plumb-line his gaze seems to be measuring the deepest
point of the pond.

He looks to one side, then backwards: not a bush, not a blade of
grass is forgotten,

then swiftly he has reached for his belt

and holds a little bottle in his hand.

Hardly has his ear convinced him than there is a hissing sound in
the glass,

hardly has his eye glimpsed something like the scurrying of a
spider than

hiss! It leaps with a whistling sound and - hui! - it drops down
beside the crown of the lily.

The water hisses and foams, the moss-green limbs stretch out,

And backwards, backwards, without stopping

the horse-dealer hurtles through the forest.

Only in a clearing where the air toys with the herby fragrance of
the berries

and the festive sound from the nearby dome

is borne on golden wings, does he sink sobbing to his knees,

his hands clasped together, so tightly, so very tightly.

Rarely has a sigh split the heart to its very depths like this.

Whatever this sigh is carrying, it must be coming like a fervent kiss.

And tears, pearl upon pearl, creep down the brown cheeks.

This must be how the Prodigal Son lay at his father's feet.

Then suddenly the praying man starts up and clutches at his belt,
then feels again.

With a muffled clinking sound he leaps up from the ground like a
wounded lion,

and in his fingers, cramped with fear,

the dripping phial is steaming.

V

Deep, deep night. Only the secret gnawing of the mouse making
a rattling noise on the coffer.

The horizon a leaking sieve, out of which coal-dust shakes itself.

Dreams pass by, heavy as lead and light as mist, around down and scattered powder:

the gaunt poet all in gold, the skinny nag rolling about in the hay,

the bride dreaming of her garland, the warrior of his helmet,

and the rascal of the rope.

In that room, softly shaded by the dark grey of the windows,

can you hear a trickling sound, as though the air were bringing fine dust from the steppe?

and a buzzing, as though a fly imprisoned in a glass were murmuring?

Perhaps the sand running away in an hour-glass, or a little mouse squeaking in the quick-lime?

So sharp it is, so penetrating,

like the whetting of a scythe upon a stone.

And on that slope, phosphorous light, such as sick limbs produce,

a greenish radiance that tangles and tingles with a hundred threads, like down,

shapeless, only in the midst of it a tiny glow where the fibres spring up,

hurling themselves with a melodious rustling sound

against the walls of the phial, and above that,

where the light fades away, a dark eye gleams.

And it goes on creeping, wriggling away, gently touching the green wall of the glass,

a glowing, greedy polypus, hopelessly trying to seize its prey.

And always the eye stares this way, as if no eyelid were shading it.

Dark hair, a neck, rise slowly from the surface of the table,

then suddenly a hand closes,

and in that very moment the vision has vanished.

There is tapping along the hallway, a stamping sound like a man's footsteps in soft shoes.

Carefully feeling his way along the wall, someone is seeking counsel,

then softly the lock of the door clicks, the bolts squeak as they are released.

Through the chamber, trembling, shyly, pours a streak of muted light,

and framed in the doorway, enveloped in a fragrance,

stands the horse-dealer in his night attire.

How gnarled and harsh-sinewed has that sturdy form become!

How many, many grey hairs cast shadows at the edge of his brow!

Oh, those folds about his mouth where lurk traces of his grief!

Thus once upon a time must the sullen prophet have mourned by the streams of Babylon.

Thus the outlaw with no resting-place

as Salvator conceived him.[1]

Opposite, finely carved, reclines the Holy Mother with her Child,

who stretches out His little gilded hand from the niche in the wall,

and below that, protected by a crystal covering, decorated with a sparkling stone,

a priceless relic, a nail from the wounds of the Saviour,

where every night in His honour

a little lamp keeps watch upon the stand.

Never in all his guilt and suffering has the horse-dealer ever let a day close

without uttering a fervent sigh at this spot.

Even on his journeyings, on his nocturnal rides, when his eyes peer dimly into the distance,

he dismounts wearily from the back of his horse

and inclines his heavy head

to where the Child extends His little hands.

A timid beggar, day after day, he stands thus at the gates of heaven.

He does not make the sign of the Cross, or bend his knee. His breath knows no words of supplication,

only murmuring drunk with sleep, and intently he feels it entwining itself

through the phial which has been entrusted to his body, like a nagging, cancerous tumour to the sick man,

and in the meagre fireplace of his life is eaten up

the fuel of another year.

Now, too, at this hour he stands silent, with his knees unbent,

and only soft groaning - and look! - look how his muscles tense!

Quick! The relic! The crystal cover! He leans against the wall and he grows faint.

A fearful tug - a groan - and he has twisted the nail loose

and forces it right before the holy shrine

into the phial's seal.

Ah! the cork cracks, ah! and the bottle falls into a million pieces,

with a whimpering here, a whimpering there, and the fluttering of spidery feet.

There's a hacking and a tingling in pursuit of the man who moans beneath the sacred image,

until, fibre by fibre, the light goes out, and the final breath of the very centre fades away.

Then mounting on the divine lamp appears the head of the horse-dealer,

white as snow.

[1]The reference is to the seventeenth century Italian painter, Salvator Rosa. The immediately preceding reference to the 'sullen prophet' is to Isaiah, who predicted the fall of Babylon. (*Isaiah* 46)

VI

Woe! a tempest of bells! A clash of trumpets! Sparks rustle through the alleyways.

The terrified mob pushes and spirals in a jumbled mass.

Heat blazes up against the gable. The sound of braying screams forth from stable and barns.

The bucket flies up and down, children weep, pushed this way and that,

and dawn breaks hesitatingly,

alight with a double glow.

It was first cock-crow when all the citizens were stirred,

with hailstorms screeching, crack after crack. There never was so terrible a storm, and the tumult formed into a ball precisely over the roof of the wealthy Bohemian, the horse-dealer,

where lightning zig-zagged down, flash after flash, with deafening crashes.

Now everywhere, in the barns and in the house,

the hedge of flame pelts forth.

In the courtyard the servants run cursing to and fro with axes and hatchets, demanding to

know who had bolted the doors from inside. They won't move and are on fire.

"The master! The master!" comes the cry from all sides. "Where is the master?"

May God have mercy on him! The fire is licking at his chamber window behind the locked panes

and the staircase to the upper room

has just come crashing into the entrance-hall

There is horrified murmuring racing all about and swelling into the waves of people,

then everything is dead silent, and they stand with foreheads grimly furrowed.

Thus once upon a time did the sons of the South gather round the stakes.

"That's the thief there whose cow attracted someone with its foreign beauty

and, barely had it been sold,

than it lay dead in its stall on the third day.

The trickster is burning, out of whose belt there came a strange ringing sound,

so that on pitch-black nights he could be recognized by his belt,

who never entered a church, never bowed before any holy image,

and whenever he encountered any Christian soul stammered in a swoon and turned pale.

In the element sent by God,

the horse-dealer is burning, along with the dome itself."

VII

On the sloping meadow stands a lime tree, its branches swaying so sweetly,

on every bough a bird's nest and a ring of bees around each blossom.

It seems to be smiling at the gloomy fir-forest out of its flowering chalices,

and blowing a hummed 'Ave' towards the Angelus from the nearby village.

And for the nearby graveyard, too,

it has sweetened the western breeze.

And it scatters petal after petal from its blossoming branch upon the forehead of the old man

who leans his head with its seething brain upon the mossy ground.

His staff is lying at his side, and his rucksack, filled with crusts,

and here and there shadowy figures dance over it with elfin steps,

as though they have slipped from the most secret protection of his breast

into a feverish heat.

He sees the village green of his childhood: playing in the branches of the linden tree,

his sweet homeland, and the heads of his parents on the pillows of their death-bed.

What he lost and strove for, the sins he committed and the suffering he endured,

how one night his hair turned white, and his own servants beat him.

Oh, that night that took from him his honour, strength, and all his goods -

and gave to him his soul!

He sees his lined face reflected in the mirror of the water,

how he never recognized himself, and then began to weep like a child.

Ah, all the tears which afterwards flowed from the deepest source -

did they unite him with the Blood of Christ? open the gates of heaven to him?

To be sure, he endured a heavy burden with patience,

but not willingly, through his own guilt.

A sick old man at forty years, he slipped from land to land,

heard his name cursed and shyly stepped to one side.

He took the beggar's crust from many a hand that once had served him

and crept, a sick man unto death, to the top of this hill,

to this hill, Almighty God!

He shudders. On New Year's Eve!

The pine forest, the deserted house - there stood the priest, there in the little garden.

Ah! in his hour of death his errant feet have brought him to this place.

This is no phantom, this one here.

Here St Michael stretches out his wings. Here on the plinth the dragon crawls

and raises its claw towards the hill.

The old man's eyes grow dark, and wildly the agony wells up in his head.

The Book, the Book -he sees the Book! Oh, Mother of God, have mercy, mercy!

He loved you, loved you in sin and shame.

The symbols turn around in circles like a wheel.

God, oh God! He sees a little hand stretch down, and

with His soft, gold touch erase the blood-drenched letters.

And on the pale mouth of the horse-dealer arises at that hour a smile.

At midday the grass-cutter lifted him up from the trunk of the linden tree

and in the waggon filled with clippings pushed him to the mortuary.

A rough stone was made for him at the expense of the parish.

The slow, short chiming of the bell accompanied him to his grave,

above which fold the angel's wings,

and where no dragon's claw can reach him.

SOME SUGGESTIONS FOR FURTHER READING

❁

Readers of this volume may wish to read the poems in German; the following editions are likely to be available in university libraries and possibly through major public libraries.

Historisch-Kritische Ausgabe, Werke, Briefwechsel. The complete works of Annette von Droste-Hülshoff, including much of the most significant correspondence, in the 14- volume critical edition published by Niemeyer (Tübingen), 1978ff. This is a formidable achievement, the culmination of many years of research by a group of scholars headed by Winfried Woesler.

A compact and very reliable edition in a single volume is that by Clemens Heselhaus, Munich 1984. This should be readily available, likewise earlier versions by Clemens Heselhaus and the two volumes edited by Bodo Plachta and Winfried Woesler, published by Insel, Frankfurt and Leipzig, 2004. (The poems in the present volume are based on these two editions.)

A selection of her poems is contained in the volume by Margaret Atkinson in the Clarendon German Series, London 1968, which also offers a brief but very helpful introduction, and some useful notes. For reasons of space, few of the ballads are included.

Readers of English have three volumes readily available to them, all of which serve as useful introductions to Annette von Droste-Hülshoff's life and work, and her place in the literary context. They are very different in intention and execution, but, taken together, they prove to be complementary to one another and extraordinarily illuminating. These are, listed in chronological order:

Margaret Mare, *Annette von Droste-Hülshoff*, London 1965.

Mary E Morgan, *Annette von Droste-Hülshoff. A Biography*, New York, 1984.

John Guthrie, *Annette von Droste-Hülshoff. A German Poet between Romanticism and Realism*, Oxford, New York, Munich 1989.

Two volumes already published by Memoirs may be seen as the companion volumes to this one:

Marion Tymms: *God's Sorely-tested Child* (A complete translation of her Spiritual Cycle, with introduction and notes) 2012, and *The Wild Muse* (A selection of her poems in translation, with introductions and brief commentaries) 2013.

Finally, in this highly selective list, which makes no claims to be a bibliography, readers of German are directed to just three books which may be of interest in very different ways, and which are likely to open up many much wider areas of reading on Droste-Hülshoff and her work. They are offered here with some hesitation and in the knowledge that they cannot possibly be more than tentative guidance in a field occupied by some of the giants of German literary scholarship (Friedrich Gundolf, Benno von Wiese, Emil Staiger, Clemens Heselhaus, to name but four) and by scholars of the later generations who have opened up totally new perspectives on her.

Peter Berglar: *Annette von Droste-Hülshoff*, Hamburg 1967. Like so many of the volumes in the series of Rowohlt Monographien, this apparently modest little paperback contains a wealth of interesting material, full of detail and packed with illustrations and information.

Ronald Schneider: *Annette von Droste-Hülshoff*, Stuttgart and Weimar, 1995. This is the second edition of Ronald Schneider's volume in the invaluable Realien zur Literatur series published by Metzler, and it represents a substantial increase in material and depth on the earlier version (1977). It is an excellent guide through the works of Droste-Hülshoff, with detailed and well-judged evaluations of them. In accordance with the intention of the series, it offers balanced guidance through the critical literature, highlights the current (at 1995) state of research and points the way forward. It is a densely written and indispensable guide for anyone wishing to pursue the subject.

Barbara Beuys: *Blamieren mag ich mich nicht. Das Leben der Annette von Droste-Hülshoff*, Frankfurt and Leipzig, 1999. This is an entertaining paperback, which offers a very modern and, as the title - a quotation from the poet herself - perhaps suggests, a very personal account of her life and the background to her work. The wealth of very varied detail is at times somewhat overwhelming, but, that said, it represents a thoroughly worthwhile companion to Ronald Schneider's measured volume.

Last Words

My dear ones, do not weep a tear for me
when my spirit has departed,
for where I am is peace
and there eternal day shines on me.

When all earthly cares have vanished,
your image will remain with me,
and I shall beg for healing for you,
for your wounds and for your pain.

And if at night across the world
peace wafts its seraph's wings,
then think no longer of my mound,
for I shall greet you from the stars.

Annette von Droste-Hülshoff, written shortly
before her death in May 1848.